RAY'S DAUGHTER

A Story of Manila

GENERAL CHARLES KING

1st WORLD
LIBRARY
Literary Society

Ray's Daughter

Charles King

© 1st World Library, 2007
PO Box 2211
Fairfield, IA 52556
www.1stworldlibrary.com
First Edition

LCCN: 2007930730

Softcover ISBN: 978-1-4218-4804-4
Hardcover ISBN: 978-1-4218-4707-8
eBook ISBN: 978-1-4218-4901-0

Purchase *"Ray's Daughter"*
as a traditional bound book at:
www.1stWorldLibrary.com/purchase.asp?ISBN=978-1-4218-4804-4

1st World Library is a literary, educational organization
dedicated to:

- Creating a free internet library of downloadable ebooks

- Hosting writing competitions and offering book publishing
scholarships.

Interested in more 1st World Library books? contact:
literacy@1stworldlibrary.com
Check us out at: www.1stworldlibrary.com

1ˢᵗ World Library Literary Society

Giving Back to the World

"If you want to work on the core problem, it's early school literacy."

- James Barksdale, former CEO of Netscape

"No skill is more crucial to the future of a child, or to a democratic and prosperous society, than literacy."

- Los Angeles Times

"Literacy... means far more than learning how to read and write... The aim is to transmit... knowledge and promote social participation."

- UNESCO

"Literacy is not a luxury, it is a right and a responsibility. If our world is to meet the challenges of the twenty-first century we must harness the energy and creativity of all our citizens."

- President Bill Clinton

"Parents should be encouraged to read to their children, and teachers should be equipped with all available techniques for teaching literacy, so the varying needs and capacities of individual kids can be taken into account."

- Hugh Mackay

CHAPTER I

The long June day was drawing to its close. Hot and strong the slanting sunbeams beat upon the grimy roofs of the train and threw distorted shadows over the sand and sage-brush that stretched to the far horizon. Dense and choking, from beneath the whirring wheels the dust-clouds rose in tawny billows that enveloped the rearmost coaches and, mingling with the black smoke of the "double-header" engines, rolled away in the dreary wake. East and west, north and south, far as the eye could reach, hemmed by low, dun-colored ridges or sharply outlined crests of remote mountain range, in lifeless desolation the landscape lay outspread to the view. Southward, streaked with white fringe of alkali, the flat monotone of sand and ashes blended with the flatter, flawless surface of a wide-spreading, ash-colored inland lake, its shores dotted at intervals with the bleaching bones of cattle and ridged with ancient wagon-tracks unwashed by not so much as a single drop from the cloudless heavens since their first impress on the sinking soil. Here and there along the right of way—a right no human being would care to dispute were the way ten times its width—some drowsing lizards, sprawling in the sunshine along the ties, roused at the sound and tremor of the coming train to squirm off into the sage-brush, but no sign of animation had been seen since the crossing of the big divide near Promontory. The long, winding train, made up of mail-, express-, baggage-, emigrant-, and smoking-cars, "tourists' coaches," and huge sleepers at the rear, with a "diner" midway in the chain, was packed with gasping humanity westward bound for the far Pacific— the long, long, tortuous climb to the snow-capped Sierras ahead, the parched and baking valley of the Great Salt Lake long, dreary miles behind. It was early June of the year '98, and the war with Spain was on.

There had been some delay at Ogden. The trains from the East over the Union Pacific and the Denver and Rio Grande came in crowded, and the resources of the Southern Pacific were suddenly taxed beyond the expectation of its officials. Troops had been whirling westward throughout the week, absorbing much of the rolling stock, and the empty cars were being rushed east again from Oakland pier, but the nearest were still some hundreds of miles from this point of transfer when a carload of recruits was dumped upon the broad platform, and the superintendent scratched his head, and screwed up the corner of his mouth, and asked an assistant how in a hotter place than even Salt Lake Valley the road could expect him to forward troops without delay "when the road took away the last car in the yard getting those Iowa boys out."

"There ain't nuthin' left 'cept that old tourist that's been rustin' and kiln-dryin' up 'longside the shops since last winter," said the junior helplessly. "Shall we have her out?"

"Guess you'll have to," was the answer. "It's that or nothin';" and the boss turned on his heel and slammed the office door behind him. "Ten to one," said he, "there'll be a kick comin' when the boys see what they've got to ride in, an' I'll let Jim take the kick."

The kick had come as predicted, but availed nothing. A score of lusty young patriots were the performers, but, being destined for service in the regulars, they had neither Senator nor State official to "wire" to in wrathful protest, as was usual on such occasions. The superintendent would have thought twice before ever suggesting that car as a component part of the train bearing the volunteers from Nebraska, Colorado, or Iowa so recently shipped over the road. "They could have made it hot for the management," said he. But these fellows, these waifs, were from no State or place in particular. They hadn't even an officer with them, but were hurrying on to their destination under command of a veteran gunner, "lanced" for the purpose at the recruiting station. He had done his best for his men. Ruefully they looked through the dust-covered interior and inspected the muddy trucks and brake-gear. "She wheezes like she had bronchitis," said the corporal, "and the inside's a cross between a hen-coop and coal-bin. You ain't going to run that old rookery for a car, are you?"

"Best we've got," was the curt reply. Yet the yardman shook his head as he heard the squeal of the rusty journals, and ordered his men to pack in fresh waste and "touch 'em up somehow." Any man who had spent a week about a railway could have prophesied "hot boxes" before that coach had run much more than its own length, but it wouldn't do for an employee to say so. The corporal looked appealingly at his fellow-passengers of the Rio Grande train. There were dozens of them stretching their legs and strolling about the platform, after getting their hand-luggage transferred and seats secured, but there was no one in position or authority to interpose. Some seemed to feel no interest.

"Get your rations and plunder aboard," he ordered, turning suddenly to his party, and, loading up with blankets, overcoats, haversacks, and canteens, the recruits speedily took possession of their new quarters, forced open the jammed windows to let out the imprisoned and overheated air, piled their boxes of hard bread and stacks of tinned meat at the ends and their scant soldier goods and chattels in the rude sections, then tumbled out again upon the platform to enjoy, while yet there was time, the freedom of the outer air, despite the torrid heat of the mid-day sunshine.

In knots of three or four they sauntered about, their hands deep in their empty pockets, their boyish eyes curiously studying the signs and posters, or wistfully peering through the screened doors at the temptations of the bar and lunch counter or the shaded windows of the dining-room, where luckier fellow-passengers were taking their fill of the good cheer afforded. Two of the number, dressed like the rest in blue flannel shirts, with trousers of lighter hue and heavier make, fanning their heated faces with their drab, broad-brimmed campaign hats, swung off the rear end of the objectionable car, and, with a quick glance about them, started briskly down the track to where the "diner" and certain sleepers of the Southern Pacific were being shunted about.

"Come back here, you fellers!" shouted the corporal, catching sight of the pair. "You don't know how soon this here train may start. Come back, I say," he added emphatically, as the two, looking first into each other's eyes, seemed to hesitate. Then, with sullen, down-cast face the nearer turned and slowly obeyed. The other, a bright, merry youngster, whose white teeth gleamed as he laughed his reply, still stood in his tracks.

"We're only going to the dining-car, corporal," he shouted. "That's going with us, so we can't be left."

"You've got no business in the dining-car, Mellen; that's not for your sort, or mine, for that matter," was the corporal's ultimatum. And with a grin still expanding his broad mouth, the recruit addressed as Mellen came reluctantly sauntering in the trail of his comrade, who had submitted in silence and yet not without a shrug of protest. It was to the latter the corporal spoke when the two had rejoined their associates.

"You've got sense enough to know you're not wanted at that diner, Murray, whether Mellen has or not. That's no place for empty pockets. What took you there?"

"Wanted a drink, and you said 'keep away from the bar-room,'" answered Murray briefly, his gray eyes glancing about from man to man in the group, resting for just a second on the form and features of one who stood a little apart, a youth of twenty-one years probably. "It was Foster's treat," he added, and that remark transferred the attention of the party at the instant to the youngster on the outskirts.

He had been leaning with folded arms against a lamp-post, looking somewhat wearily up the long platform to where in pairs or little groups the passengers were strolling, men and women both, seeking relief from the constraint and stiffness of the long ride by rail. He had an interesting—even a handsome—face, and his figure was well knit, well propor-tioned. His eyes were a dark, soft brown, with very long, curving lashes, his nose straight, his mouth finely curved, soft and sensitive. His throat was full, round, and at the base very white and fair, as the unfastened and flapping shirt-collar now enabled one to see. His hands, too, were soft and white, showing that at least one of the twenty came not from the ranks of the toilers. His shoes were of finer make than those of his comrades, and the handkerchief so loosely knotted at the opening of the coarse blue shirt was of handsome and costly silk. He had been paying scant attention to his surroundings, and was absorbed, evidently, in his watch on the tourists up the platform when recalled to himself by the consciousness that all eyes were upon him.

"What's this about your treatin', Foster?" asked the corporal.

For a week he had felt sure the boy had money, and not a little. Nothing would have persuaded him to borrow a cent of Foster or anybody else, but others, and plenty of them, had no such scruples.

The young recruit turned slowly. He seemed reluctant to quit his scrutiny of his fellow-passengers. The abrupt tone and manner of the accustomed regular, too, jarred upon him. It might be the corporal's prerogative so to address his charges, but this one didn't like it, and meant to show that he didn't. His money at least was his own, and he could do with it as he liked. The answer did not come until the question had been asked twice. Then in words as brief and manner as blunt he said,—

"Why shouldn't I?"

Corporal Connelly stood a second or two without venturing a word, looking steadfastly at the young soldier, whose attitude was unchanged and whose eyes were again fixed on the distant group, as though in weary disdain of those about him. Then Connelly took half a dozen quick, springy steps that landed him close to the unmoved recruit.

"You've two things to learn among two thousand, Foster," said he in low, firm voice. "One is to keep your money, and the other, your temper. I spoke for your good principally, but if you've been ladling out your money to be spent in liquor, I say stop it. There's to be no whiskey in that car."

"Nobody wants it less than I do," said Foster wearily. "Why didn't you keep it out of the others?"

"Because I never knew till it was gone. How much money

did you give Murray—and why?" and Connelly's eyes were looking straight into those of Foster as he spoke, compelling respect for sturdy manhood.

"A dollar, I believe," was the languid answer, "and because he asked it." And again the lad's gaze wandered off along the platform.

The switch engine was busily at work making up the train, and brakemen were signalling up and down the line. The dining-car, followed by some ponderous sleepers, came gliding slowly along the rails and brought up with a bump and jar against the buffers of the old tourists' ark assigned the recruits. Somewhere up at the thronged station a bell began to jangle, followed by a shout of "All aboard!"

"Tumble in, you men," ordered Connelly, and at the moment there came a general movement of the crowd in their direction. The passengers of the sleepers were hurrying to their assigned places, some with flushed faces and expostulation. They thought their car should have come to them.

"It's because our train is so very long," explained the brakeman to some ladies whom he was assisting up the steps. "We've twice as many cars as usual. Yours is the next car, ma'am; the one behind the diner."

The recruit, Foster, had started, but slowly, when in obedience to the corporal's order his fellows began to move. He was still looking, half in search, half in expectation, towards the main entrance of the station building. But the instant he became aware of the movement in his direction on the part of the passengers he pushed ahead past several of the party; he even half shoved aside one of their number who had just grasped the hand-rail of the car, then sprang lightly past him and disappeared within the door-way. There, half hidden by the gloom of the interior, he stood well back from the grimy windows, yet peering intently through at the swiftly passing crowd.

Suddenly he stooped, recoiled, and seated himself in the opposite section while his comrades came filing rapidly in, and at the moment a tall young officer in dark uniform, a man perhaps of twenty-five, with a singularly handsome face and form, strode past the window, scrupulously acknowledged Connelly's salute, and then, glancing about, saw the heads and shoulders of a dozen soldiers at the windows.

"Why, what detachment is this, corporal?" he asked. "We brought no troops on our train."

"Recruits—th Cavalry, sir," was the ready answer. "We came by way of Denver."

"Ah, yes; that explains it. Who's in command?" And the tall officer looked about him as though in search of kindred rank.

"We have no officer with us, sir," said Connelly diplomatically. "I'm—in charge."

"You'll have to hurry, sir," spoke the brakeman at the moment. "Jump on the diner, if you like, and go through."

The officer took the hint and sprang to the steps. There he turned and faced the platform again just as the train began to move.

A little group, two ladies and a man of middle age, stood directly opposite him, closely scanning the train, and all on a sudden their faces beamed, their glances were directed, their hands waved towards him.

"Good-by! Good-by! Take good care of yourself! Wire from Sacramento!" were their cries, addressed apparently to his head, and turning quickly, he found himself confronting a young girl standing smiling on the platform of the dining-car, her tiny feet about on a level with his knees; yet he had hardly to cast an upward glance, for her beaming, beautiful face was but a trifle higher than his own. In all his life he had never seen one so pretty.

Realizing that he stood between this fair traveller and the friends who were there to wish her god-speed; recognizing, too, with the swift intuition of his class, the possibility of establishing relations on his own account, the young soldier snatched off his new forage-cap, briefly said, "I beg your pardon; take my place," and, swinging outward, transferred himself to the rear of the recruit car, thereby causing the corporal to recoil upon a grinning squad of embryo troopers who were shouting jocular farewell to the natives, and getting much in the way of train-hands who were busy straightening out the bell-cord.

Something seemed amiss with that portion of it which made part of the equipment of the old tourists' car. It was either wedged in the narrow orifice above the door or caught among the rings of the pendants from above, for it resisted every jerk, whereat the brakeman set his teeth and said improper things. It would have grieved the management to hear this faithful employe's denunciation of that particular item of their rolling-stock.

"Get out of the way here, boys, and let's see what's the matter with this damned bell-cord," he continued, elbowing his way through the swarm about the door. Once fairly within, he threw a quick glance along the aisle. The left sections of the car were deserted. Out of almost every window on the right side poked a head and pair of blue flannel shoulders.

Only one man of the party seemed to have no further interest in what was going on outside. With one hand still grasping the edge of the upright partition between two sections near the forward end, and the other just letting go, apparently, of the bell-cord, the tall, slender, well-built young soldier, with dark-brown eyes and softly curling lashes, was lowering himself into the aisle. The brakeman proceeded to rebuke him on the spot.

"Look here, young feller, you'll have to keep your hands off that bell-cord. Here I've been cussin' things for keeps, thinking it was knotted or caught. It was just you had hold of it. Don't you know better'n that? Ain't you ever travelled before?"

The man addressed was stowing something away inside the breast of his shirt. He did it with almost ostentatious deliberation, quietly eying the brakeman before replying. Then, slowly readjusting the knot of a fine black-silk necktie, so that its broad, flapping ends spread over the coarser material of the garment, he slowly looked the justly exasperated brakeman over from head to foot and as slowly and placidly answered:

"Not more than about half around the world. As for your bell-cord, it was knotted; it caught in that ring. I saw that someone was tugging and trying to get it loose, so I swung up there and straightened it. Just what you'd have done under the circumstances, I fancy."

The brakeman turned redder under the ruddy brown of his sun-tanned skin. This was no raw "rookie" after all. In his own vernacular, as afterwards expressed to the conductor, "I seen I was up ag'in' the real t'ing dis time," but it was hard to admit it at the moment. Vexation had to have a vent. The bell-cord no longer served. The supposed meddler had proved a help. Something or somebody had to be the victim of the honest brakeman's spleen, so, somewhat unluckily, as events determined, he took it out on the company and that decrepit car, now buzzing along with much complaint of axle and of bearing.

"Damn this old shake-down, anyhow!" said he. "The company ought to know 'nough not to have such things lyin' round loose. Some night it'll fall to pieces and kill folks." And with this implied apology for his aspersions of Recruit Foster, the brakeman bustled away.

But what he said was heard by more than one, and remembered when perhaps he would have wished it forgotten. The delay at Ogden was supplemented by a long halt before the setting of that blazing sun, necessitated by the firing of the waste in the boxes of those long-neglected trucks. Far back as the rearmost sleeper the sickening smell of burning, oil-steeped packing drove feminine occupants to their satchels in search of scent-bottles, and the men to such comfort as could be found in flasks of bulkier make.

In the heart of the desert, with dust and desolation spreading far on every hand, the long train had stopped to douse those foul-smelling fires, and, while train-hands pried off the red-hot caps and dumped buckets of water into the blazing cavities, changing malodorous smoke to dense clouds of equally unsavory steam, and the recruits in the afflicted car found consolation in "joshing" the hard-sweating, hard-swearing workers, the young officer who had boarded the second sleeper at Ogden, together with half a dozen bipeds in dusters or frazzled shirt-sleeves, had become involved in a complication on the shadier side of the train.

Somewhere into the sage-brush a jack-rabbit had darted and was now in hiding. With a dozen eager heads poked from the northward windows and stretching arms and index fingers guiding them in their inglorious hunt, the lieutenant and his few associates were stalking the first four-footed object sighted from the train since the crossing of the bald divide.

Within the heated cars, with flushed faces and plying palm-leaf fans, a few of the women passengers were languidly gazing from the windows. At the centre window of the second sleeper, without a palm-leaf and looking serene and unperturbed, sat the young girl whose lovely face had so excited Mr. Stuyvesant's deep admiration. Thrice since leaving Ogden, on one pretext or other, had he passed her section and stolen such a look as could be given without obvious staring. Immediately in rear of the seat she occupied was an austere maiden of middle age, one of the passengers who had come on by the Union Pacific from Omaha. Directly opposite sat two men whom Stuyvesant had held in but scant esteem up to the time they left the valley of Salt Lake. Now, because their sections stood over against hers, his manner relaxed with his mood. Circumstances had brought the elderly maid and himself to the same table on two occasions in the dining-car, but he had hitherto felt no desire to press the acquaintance.

This afternoon he minded him of a new book he had in his bag, for literature, he judged, might be her hobby, and had engaged her in conversation, of which his share was meant to impress the tiny, translucent ear that nestled in the dark-brown coils and waves of the pretty head in front of him.

When, however, it became patent that his companion desired to form her own impressions of the pages uninfluenced by his well-delivered comments, Mr. Stuyvesant had bethought him of the semi-somnolent occupants of the opposite section, and some cabalistic signs he ventured with a little silver cup summoned them in pleased surprise to the water-cooler at the rear end, where he regaled them with a good story and the best of V. O. P. Scotch, and accepted their lavish bid to sit with them awhile.

From this coign of vantage he had studied her sweet, serious, oval face as she sat placidly reading a little volume in her lap, only once in a while raising a pair of very dark, very beautiful, very heavily browed and lashed brown eyes for brief survey of the forbidding landscape; then, with never an instant's peep at him, dropping their gaze again upon the book.

Not once in the long, hot afternoon had she vouchsafed him the minimum of a show of interest, curiosity, or even consciousness of his presence. Then the train made its second stop on account of the fires, and Bre'r Rabbit his luckless break into the long monotony of the declining day.

Tentative spikes, clods, and empty flasks having failed to find him, the beaters had essayed a skirmish line, and with instant result. Like a meteoric puff of gray and white, to a chorus of yells and the accompaniment of a volley of missiles, Jack had shot into space from behind his shelter and darted zigzagging through the brush. A whizzing spike, a chance shot that nearly grazed his nose, so dazzled his brainlet that the terrified creature doubled on his trail and came bounding back towards the train.

Close to the track-side ran a narrow ditch. In this ditch at the instant crouched the tall lieutenant. Into this ditch leaped Bunny, and the next second had whizzed past the stooping form and bored straight into a little wooden drain. There some unseen, unlooked-for object blocked him.

Desperately the hind-legs kicked and tore in the effort to force the passage, and with a shout of triumph the tall soldier swooped upon the prize, seized the struggling legs, swung the wretched creature aloft, and for the first time in six mortal hours met full in his own the gaze of the deep, beautiful brown eyes he had so striven to attract, and they were half pleading, half commanding for Bunny. The next instant, uninjured, but leaping madly for life, Bre'r Rabbit was streaking eastward out of harm's way, a liberated victim whose first huge leap owed much of its length to the impetus of Stuyvesant's long, lean, sinewy arm.

This time when he looked up and raised his cap, and stood there with his blond hair blowing down over his broad white forehead, although the soft curves of the ripe red lips at the window above him changed not, there was something in the dark-brown eyes that seemed to say "Thank you!"

Yet when he would have met those eyes again that evening, when "Last call for dinner in the dining-car" was sounding through the train, he could not. Neither were they among those that peered from between parted curtains in the dim light of the sleeper, many in fright, all in anxiety, when somewhere in the dead of the summer night, long after all occupants of the rearmost cars were wrapped in slumber, the long train bumped to sudden jarring standstill, and up ahead there arose sound of rush, of excitement and alarm.

CHAPTER II

It was just after sunset when, for the second time, the hot boxes of the recruit car had been treated to liberal libations from the water-tank, and the belated train again moved on.

Dinner had been ready in the dining-car a full hour, but so long as the sickening smell of burning waste arose from the trucks immediately in front very few of the passengers seemed capable of eating. The car, as a consequence, was crowded towards eight o'clock, and the steward and waiters were busy men.

The evening air, drifting in through open windows, was cooler than it had been during the day, but still held enough of the noontide caloric to make fans a comfort, and Mr. Stuyvesant, dining at a "four-in-hand" table well to the front, and attempting to hold his own in a somewhat desultory talk with his fellow-men, found himself paying far more attention to the lovely face of the girl across the aisle than to the viands set before him.

She was seated facing the front, and opposite the austere maiden previously mentioned. Conversation had already begun, and now Stuyvesant was able to see that, beautiful in feature as was her face in repose, its beauty was far enhanced when animated and smiling.

When to well-nigh perfect external features there is added the charm of faultlessly even and snowy teeth and a smile that illumines the entire face, shining in the eyes as it plays about the pretty, sensitive mouth, a young woman is fully equipped for conquest.

Stuyvesant gazed in fascination uncontrollable. He envied the prim, precise creature who sat unbending, severe, and, even while keeping up a semblance of interest in the conversation, seemed to feel it a duty to display disapprobation of such youthful charms.

No woman is so assured that beauty is only skin deep as she who has none of it. Her manner, therefore, had been decidedly stiff, and from that had imperceptibly advanced to condescension, but when the steward presently appeared with a siphon of iced seltzer, and, bowing deferentially, said he hoped everything was to Miss Ray's liking, and added that it seemed a long time since they had seen the captain and supposed he must be a colonel now, the thin eyebrows of the tall maiden were uplifted into little arches that paralleled the furrows of her brow as she inquired:

"Miss Ray?—from Fort Leavenworth?"

The answer was a smiling nod of assent as the younger lady buried her lovely, dark face in the flowers set before her by the assiduous waiter, and Stuyvesant felt sure she was trying to control an inclination to laugh.

"Well, you must excuse me if I have been a little—slow," said the elder in evident perturbation. "You see—we meet such queer people travelling—sometimes. Don't you find it so?"

The dark face was dimpling now with suppressed merriment.

"Yes—occasionally," was the smiling answer.

"But then, being the daughter of an army officer," pursued the other hurriedly, "you have to travel a great deal. I suppose you really—have no home?" she essayed in the half-hopeful tone to be expected of one who considered that a being so endowed by nature must suffer some compensatory discomforts.

"Yes and—no," answered Miss Ray urbanely. "In one sense we army girls have no home. In another, we have homes everywhere."

It is a reproach in the eyes of certain severe moralists that a fellow-being should be so obviously content with his or her lot. The elder woman seemed to feel it a duty to acquaint this beaming creature with the manifest deficiency in her moral make-up.

"Yes, but I should think most any one would rather have a real home, a place where they weren't bounden to anybody, no matter if it was homely." (She called it "humbly," and associated it in mind with the words of Payne's immortal song.) "Now, when I went to see Colonel Ray about our society, he told me he had to break up everything, going to Cuba, but he didn't mention about your going West."

"Father was a little low in his mind that day," said Miss Ray, a shade of sadness passing over her face. "Both my brothers are in the service, and one is barely seventeen."

"Out at service!" interrupted the other. "You don't mean—"

"No," was the laughing answer, and in Miss Ray's enjoyment of the situation her eyes came perilously near seeking those of Mr. Stuyvesant, which she well knew were fixed upon her. "I mean that both are in the army."

"Well—I thought not—still—I didn't know. It's all rather new to me, this dealin' with soldiers, but I suppose I'll get to know all about it after a spell. Our society's getting much encouraged."

"Red Cross?" queried Miss Ray, with uplifted brows and evident interest, yet a suspicion of incredulity.

"Well, same thing, only *we* don't propose to levy contributions right and left like they do. I am vice-president of the Society of Patriotic Daughters of America, you know. I thought perhaps your father might have told you. And our association is self-sustaining, at least it will be as soon as we are formally recognized by the government. You know the Red Cross hasn't any real standing, whereas our folks expect the President to issue the order right away, making us part of the regular hospital brigade. Now, your father was very encouraging, though some officers we talked to were too stuck up to be decent. When I called on General Drayton he just as much as up and told me we'd only be in the way."

Just here, it must be owned, Miss Ray found it necessary to dive under the table for a handkerchief which she had not dropped.

Mr. Stuyvesant, ignoring the teachings of his childhood and gazing over the rim of his coffee-cup, observed that she was with difficulty concealing her merriment. Then, all of a sudden, her face, that had been so full of radiance, became suddenly clouded by concern and distress. The door at the head of the car had swung suddenly open and remained so, despite the roar and racket of the wheels and the sweep of dust and cinders down the aisle. The steward glanced up from his cupboard opposite the kitchen window at the rear, and quickly motioned to some one to shut that door. A waiter sprang forward, and then came the steward himself. The look in the girl's face was enough for Stuyvesant. He whirled about to see what had caused it, and became instantly aware of a stout-built soldier swaying uneasily at the entrance and in thick tones arguing with the waiter. He saw at a glance the man had been drinking, and divined he was there to get more liquor. He was on the point of warning the steward to sell him none, but was saved the trouble. The steward bent down and whispered:

"This makes the second time he's come in since six o'clock. I refused to let him have a drop. Can't something be done to keep him out? We can't lock the door, you know, sir."

Stuyvesant quickly arose and stepped up the aisle. By this time everybody was gazing towards the front entrance in concern and curiosity. The colored waiter was still confronting the soldier as though to prevent his coming farther into the car. The soldier, with flushed and sodden face and angry eyes, had placed a hand on the broad shoulder of the servant and was clumsily striving to put him aside.

Stuyvesant's tall, athletic figure suddenly shut both from view. Never hesitating, he quickly elbowed the negro out of the way, seized the doorknob with his left hand, throwing the door wide open, then, looking the soldier full in the face, pointed to the tourist car with the other.

"Go back at once," was all he said.

The man had been hardly six days in service, and had learned little of army life or ways. He was a whole American citizen, however, if he was half drunk, and the average American thinks twice before he obeys a mandate of any kind. This one coming from a tall young swell was especially obnoxious.

The uniform as yet had little effect on Recruit Murray. Where he hailed from the sight of it had for years provoked only demonstrations of derision and dislike. He didn't know who the officer was—didn't want to know—didn't care. What he wanted was whiskey, and so long as the money was burning in his pocket he knew no reason why he shouldn't have it. Therefore, instead of obeying, he stood there, sullen and swaying, scowling up as though in hate and defiance into the grave, set young face. Another second and the thing was settled. Stuyvesant's right hand grasped the blue collar at the throat, the long, slender fingers gripping tight, and half shot, half lifted the amazed recruit across the swaying platform and into the reeling car ahead. There he plumped his captive down into a seat and sent for the corporal. Connelly came, rubbing his eyes, and took in the situation at a glance.

"I ordered him not to leave the car three hours ago, sir," he quickly spoke. "But after supper I got drowsy and fell asleep in my section. Then he skinned out. I'd iron him, sir, if I had anything of the kind."

"No," said Stuyvesant, "don't think of that. Just keep a watch over him and forbid his leaving the section. No, sir, none of that," he added, as in drunken dignity Murray was searching for a match to light his pipe and hide his humiliation. "There must be no smoking in this flimsy car, corporal. A spark would set fire to it in a second."

"Them was my orders, sir. This fellow knows it as well as I do. But he's given trouble one way or other ever since we started. You hear that again, now, Murray: no drink; no smoke. I'll see to it that he doesn't quit the car again, sir," he concluded, turning appealingly to the young officer, and Stuyvesant, taking a quiet look up and down the dimly lighted, dusty aisle, was about to return to the "diner," when Murray struggled to his feet. Balked in his hope of getting more drink, and defrauded, as in his muddled condition it seemed to him, of the solace of tobacco, the devil in him roused to evil effort by the vile liquor procured surreptitiously somewhere along the line, the time had come for him, as he judged, to assert himself before his fellows and prove himself a man.

"You think you're a better man than I am," he began thickly, glaring savagely at the young officer. "But I'll be even with you, young fellow. I'll—" And here ended the harangue, for, one broad hand clapped over the leering mouth and the other grasping the back of his collar, Corporal Connelly jammed him down on the seat with a shock that shook the car.

"Shut up, you drunken fool!" he cried. "Don't mind him, lieutenant. He's only a day at the depot, sir. Sit still, you blackguard, or I'll smash you!"—this to Murray, who, half suffocated, was writhing in his effort to escape. "A—ch!" he cried, with sudden wrenching away of the brawny hand, "the beast has bitten me," and the broad palm, dripping with blood, was held up to the light.

Deeply indented, there were the jagged marks of Murray's teeth.

"Here, Foster, Hunt, grab this man and don't let him stir, hand or foot. See what you get for giving a drunkard money. Grab him, I say!" shouted Connelly, grinning with mingled pain and wrath as the lieutenant led him to the wash-stand.

Another recruit, a stalwart fellow, who had apparently seen previous service, sprang to the aid of the first two named, and between them, though he stormed and struggled a moment, the wretch was jammed and held in his corner.

Stanching the blood as best he could and bandaging the hand

with his own kerchief, Stuyvesant bade the corporal sit at an open window a moment, for he looked a trifle faint and sick,—it was a brutal bite. But Connelly was game.

"That blackguard's got to be taught there's a God in Israel," he exclaimed, as he turned back to the rear of the car. "I beg the lieutenant's pardon, but—he is not in the regular army, I see," with a glance at the collar of the young officer's blouse. "We sometimes get hard cases to deal with, and this is one of them. This kind of a cur wouldn't hesitate to shoot an officer in the back or stab him in the dark if he didn't like him. I hope the lieutenant may never be bothered with him again. No, damn you!" he added between his set teeth, as he looked down at the sullen, scowling prisoner, "what you ought to have is a good hiding, and what you'll get, if you give any more trouble, is a roping, hand and foot. We ought to have irons on a trip like this, lieutenant," he continued, glancing up into the calm, refined face of the young soldier. "But I can get a rope, if you say so, and tie him in his berth."

"I have no authority in the matter," said Stuyvesant reflectively. "No one has but you, that I know of. Perhaps he'll be quiet when he cools down," and the lieutenant looked doubtfully at the semi-savage in the section nearest the door.

"He'll give no more trouble this night, anyhow," said Connelly, as the officer turned to go. "And thank you, sir, for this," and he held up the bandaged hand. "But I'll keep my eyes peeled whenever he's about hereafter, and you'll be wise to do the same, sir."

For one instant, as the lieutenant paused at the door-way and looked back, the eyes of the two men met, his so brave and blue and clear; the other's—Murray's—furtive, blood-shot, and full of hate. Then the door slammed and Stuyvesant was gone.

Twice again that night he visited the recruit car. At ten o'clock, after enjoying for an hour or more the sight of Miss Ray in animated chat with two of the six women passengers of the sleeper, and the sound of her pleasant voice, Stuyvesant wandered into the diner for a glass of cool Budweiser.

"That's an ugly brute of a fellow that bit your corporal, sir," said the steward. "I was in there just now, and he's as surly as a cur dog yet."

Stuyvesant nodded without a word. He was in a petulant frame of mind. He wanted "worst kind," as he would have expressed it, to know that girl, but not a glance would she give him. She owed him one, thought he, for letting that rabbit go. Moreover, being an army girl, as he had learned, she should not be so offish with an officer.

Then the readiness with which the corporal had "spotted" him as a volunteer, as not a regular, occurred to him, and added to his faintly irritable mood. True, his coat-collar bore the tell-tale letters U. S. V., but he had served some years with one of the swellest of swell Eastern regiments, whose set-up and style were not excelled by the regulars, whose officers prided themselves upon their dress and bearing.

If it was because he was not of the regular service that Miss Ray would not vouchsafe him a glance, Mr. Stuyvesant was quite ready to bid her understand he held himself as high as any soldier in her father's famous corps. If it was not that, then what in blazes was it?

He knew that in travelling cross continent in this way it was considered the proper thing for an officer of the regular army to send his card by the porter to the wife or daughter of any brother officer who might be aboard, and to tender such civilities as he would be glad to have paid his own were he so provided. He wondered whether it would do to send his pasteboard with a little note to the effect that he had once met Colonel Ray at the United Service Club, and would be glad to pay his respects to the colonel's daughter.

It was an unusual thing for Mr. Stuyvesant to quaff beer at any time, except after heavy exercise at polo or tennis, but to-night he was ruffled, and when the porter began making up the berths and dames and damsels disappeared, he had wandered disconsolately into the diner and ordered beer as his excuse. Then he crossed the platform and entered the tourist.

The night was hot and close. The men were lying two in a berth, as a rule, the upper berths not being used.

One or two, Murray among them, had not removed their trousers, but most of them were stretched out in their undergarments, while others, chatting in low tones, were watching the brakeman turning down the lights. They made way respectfully as the lieutenant entered. Connelly came to meet him and nodded significantly at Murray, who lay in a berth near the middle of the car, still carefully watched by Hunt. Foster, wearied, had turned in, and, with his face to the window, seemed to have fallen asleep. The conductor came through, lantern in hand.

"It's the quietest and best behaved lot, barring that chap, I ever carried," said he to Stuyvesant. "But he's wicked enough for a dozen. Wonder he don't go to sleep."

"Humph! says he wants a bottle of beer," grunted Connelly. "Can't get to sleep without it. I wouldn't give it to him if I had a kag."

"He doesn't deserve it, of course," said the conductor. "What he ought to have is an all-around licking. But I've known beer to have a soothing effect on men who'd been drinking, and it might put him to sleep and save bother."

"Let him have it," said Stuyvesant briefly. "I'll send it in by the steward. And, corporal, if you or any of your men would like it, I'll be glad—"

Some two or three looked quickly and expectantly up, as though they might like it very much, but Corporal Connelly said he "dassent," he "never took a drink of anything on duty since three years ago come Fourth of July." So the others were abashed and would not ask. Older hands would not have held their tongues.

To Murray's surprise, a brimming glass of cool beer was presently offered him. He gulped it thirstily down, and without a word held out the glass for more. A grinning waiter obliged him with what remained in the bottle. Murray asked if that was all, then, with something like a grunt of dissatisfaction, rolled heavily over and turned his face to the wall.

"Well, of all the ungrateful cads I ever seen," said Hunt, "you're the worst! D'ye know who sent that beer, Murray? It was the young officer you insulted." But Murray's only answer at the moment was a demand that Hunt shut up and let him go to sleep.

The last thing Stuyvesant remembered before dozing off was that the smell of those journal-boxes was getting worse. At two in the morning, in the heart of the desert, the conductor had made his way through the train and remarked that, despite that unpleasant odor, every man of the recruit detachment was sound asleep. In a berth next the door the steward of the dining-car had found room, and the entire car seemed wrapped in repose.

Five minutes later by the watch, it was wrapped in flames.

Speaking of the matter later in the morning, the brakeman said it didn't seem ten seconds after he had pulled the bell-rope and given the alarm before Lieutenant Stuyvesant, a tall, slim figure in pajamas and slippers, came bounding to his aid.

The flames even then were bursting from under the steps and platform, the dense smoke pouring from the rear door of the recruit car, and coughing, choking, blinded, staggering, some of them scorched and blistered, most of them clad only in undershirt and drawers, the luckless young troopers came groping forth and were bundled on into the interior of the diner. Some in their excitement strove to leap from the train before it came to its bumping, grinding halt. Some were screaming in pain and panic. Only one, Hunt, was dressed throughout in uniform.

The steward of the diner, nearly suffocated before being dragged out of his berth, was making vain effort to shove a way back into the blazing car, crying that all his money was under that pillow. But it was impossible to stem the torrent of human forms.

The instant the train stopped, the flames shot upward through the skylight and ventilator, and then the voice of Connelly was heard yelling for aid. Seizing a blanket that had been dragged after him by some bewildered recruit, and throwing it over his head and shoulders, Stuyvesant, bending low, dove headlong into the dense wall of smoke.

The flames came leaping and lapping out from the door-way

the instant he disappeared, and a groan of dismay arose from the little group already gathered at the side of the track. Five, ten seconds of awful suspense, and then, bending lower still, his loose clothing afire, his hair and eyebrows singed, his face black with soot and smoke and seared by flame, the young officer came plunging forth, dragging by the legs a prostrate, howling man, and after them, blind and staggering, came Connelly.

Eager hands received and guided the rescuers, leading them into the diner, while the trainmen worked the stiff levers, broke loose the coupling, and swung their lanterns in frantic signals to the engineer, far ahead.

Another moment and the blazing car was drawn away, run up the track a hundred yards, and left to illumine the night and burn to ashes, while male passengers swarmed about the dining-car, proffering stimulant and consolation.

Besides Stuyvesant and Corporal Connelly, two soldiers were seriously burned. Every stitch of clothing not actually on their persons at the moment of their escape was already consumed, and with it every ounce of their soldier rations and supplies.

The men least injured were those who, being nearest the rear door, were first to escape. The men worst burned were those longest held within the blazing car, barring one, Murray, whom Hunt had thoughtfully bound hand and foot as he slept, reasoning that in that way only might his guardians enjoy a like blessing.

Connelly had tripped over the roaring bully as he lay on his back in the aisle. Stuyvesant had rushed in, and between them they dragged him to a place of safety. There, his limbs unbound, his tongue unloosed, Murray indulged in a blast of malediction on the road, the company, the government, his comrades, even his benefactors, and then thoughtfully demanded drink. There was no longer a stern corporal to forbid, for Connelly, suffering and almost sightless, had been led into a rear coach. But there was no longer money with which to buy, for Foster's last visible cent had gone up in smoke and flame, and, scorched and smarting in a dozen places, wrapped in a blanket in lieu of clothes, the dark-eyed young soldier sat, still trembling from excitement, by the roadside.

It was three hours before the wreck could be cleared, another car procured, and the recruits bundled into it. Then, as dawn was spreading over the firmament, the train pushed on, and the last thing Gerard Stuyvesant was conscious of before, exhausted, he dropped off to troubled sleep, was that a soft, slender hand was renewing the cool bandage over his burning eyes, and that he heard a passenger say "That little brunette—that little Miss Ray—was worth the hull carload of women put together. She just went in and nursed and bandaged the burned men like as though they'd been her own brothers."

Certainly the young lady had been of particular service in the case of Connelly and one of the seriously injured recruits. She had done something for every man whose burns deserved attention, with a single exception.

Recruit Foster had declared himself in need of no aid, and with his face to the wall lay well out of sight.

CHAPTER III

At one of the desert stations in the Humboldt Valley a physician boarded the train under telegraphic orders from the company and went some distance up the road.

He had brought lint and bandages and soothing lotions, but in several cases said no change was advisable, that with handkerchiefs contributed by the passengers and bandages made from surplus shirts, little Miss Ray had extemporized well and had skilfully treated her bewildered patients. Questioned and complimented both, Miss Ray blushingly admitted that she had studied "First Aid to the Wounded" and had had some instructions in the post hospitals of more than one big frontier fort. Passengers had ransacked bags and trunks and presented spare clothing to the few recruits whom the garments would fit. But most of the men were shoeless and blanketed when morning dawned, and all were thankful when served with coffee and a light breakfast, though many even then were too much excited and some in too much pain to eat.

Mellen, the laughing and joyous lad of yesterday, was nursing a blistered hand and arm and stalking about the car in stocking feet and a pair of trousers two sizes too big for him. Murray, now that the corporal was no longer able to retain active command, had resumed his truculent and swaggering manner. Almost the first thing he did was to demand more money of Foster, and call him a liar when told that every dollar was burned. Then he sought to pick a fight with Hunt, who had, as he expressed it, "roped him like a steer," but the carload by this time had had too much of his bluster and made common cause against him.

Two brawny lads gave him fair warning that if he laid a finger on Hunt they would "lay him out." Then he insisted on seeing the corporal and complaining of ill-treatment. And with such diversion the long day wore on.

Stuyvesant, refreshed by several hours of sleep, yet looking somewhat singed and blistered, went through the car to see the sufferers along towards eleven o'clock. He had inquired of the porter for Miss Ray, who was not visible when he had finished his toilet, and was told that she had remained up until after the doctor came aboard, and was now sleeping. Finding three of the men stretched in the berths with comrades fanning them, he ordered cooling drinks compounded by the steward, and later, as they began the climb of the Sierras and the men grew hungry, he sought to get a substantial luncheon for them on the diner, but was told their supply on hand was barely sufficient for the regular passengers.

So when the train stopped at Truckee he tumbled off with three of the party, bought up a quantity of bread and cheese, soda crackers and fruit, and after consultation with the conductor wired ahead to Sacramento for a hot dinner for eighteen men to be ready at the restaurant in the station, it being now certain that they could not reach San Francisco before midnight. "The company ought to do that," said the trainmen, and "the company" had authorized the light breakfast tendered earlier in the day. In view of the fact that every item of personal property in possession of the recruits had been destroyed, together with every crumb of their rations, nobody questioned that the company would only be too glad to do that much for the men so nearly burned alive in their travelling holocaust.

Not a doubt was entertained among either passengers or trainmen as to the origin of the fire. It had started underneath, and the dry woodwork burned like tinder, and what was there to cause it but those blazing boxes on the forward truck? The conductor knew there had been no smoking aboard the car, and that every man was asleep when he went through at two o'clock. The brakeman had prophesied disaster and danger. It was God's mercy that warned the poor fellows in time.

Not until along in the afternoon, as they were spinning swiftly down through the marvellous scenery about Blue Canon and Cape Horn, did Miss Ray again appear. Stuyvesant had been sitting awhile by Connelly, and had arranged with him to wire to the Presidio for ambulances to meet the party at Oakland Pier, for two at least would be unable to walk, and, until provided with shoes and clothing, few could march the distance. Then he had spent a few minutes with the other patients.

When he returned to the sleeper there at last was the object of so many of his thoughts. But she was reclining wearily, her head upon a pillow, and the austere maid and two other women stood guard over her. "A severe headache," was the explanation, and Stuyvesant felt that he must defer his intrusion until later.

Somewhere down the western slope of the Sierras he found at a station some delicious cherries, and a little basket of the choicest he made bold to send with his compliments and the hope that her indisposition would soon disappear. The porter came back with the lady's thanks. The cherries were "lovely," but Stuyvesant observed that not more than one or two found their way to those pearly teeth, the rest being devoured by her too devoted attendants.

It was after nine at night when he marshalled his motley party into the dining-room at Sacramento and they were made glad by substantial, well-cooked food, with abundant hot coffee. They thanked him gratefully, did many of the young fellows, and hoped they might meet more such officers. An elderly passenger who had quietly noted the outlay of money to which Mr. Stuyvesant had been subjected strolled up to the manager. "That young gentleman has had to pay too much to-day. Just receipt the bill if you please," said he, and drew forth a roll of treasury notes. Stuyvesant went in search of this new benefactor when he heard of it. "There was really no necessity, sir," said he, "though I fully appreciate your kindness. The company will doubtless reimburse me for any such outlay."

"If they will reimburse you, my young friend," said the veteran traveller drily, "they'll reimburse me. At all events, I know them better than you do, and I don't intend to let you bear all the risk." The lieutenant argued, but the elder was firm. As the men shuffled back to the train with full stomachs and brightened faces, Murray hulking by them with averted eyes and Mellen tendering a grinning salute, the manager came forward. "There's one man shy, sir, even counting the dinners sent aboard," said he, and Hunt, hearing it, turned back and explained.

"It is Foster, sir. He said he wasn't hungry and couldn't eat. I reckon it's because he wouldn't turn out in such looking clothes as were given him."

Yet when Stuyvesant went to the car to see whether the young soldier could not be induced to change his mind, it was discovered that he had turned out. His berth was empty. Nor did he appear until just as the train was starting. He explained that he had stepped off on the outer side away from the crowd for a little fresh air. There was plenty of bread and cheese left from luncheon. He didn't care for anything, really. And, indeed, he seemed most anxious to get back to his berth and away from the lieutenant, in whose presence he was obviously and painfully ill at ease.

Stuyvesant turned away, feeling a trifle annoyed or hurt, he couldn't tell which, and swung himself to the platform of the sleeper as it came gliding by. At last he could hope to find opportunity to thank Miss Ray for her attention to the injured men and incidentally her ministrations on his own account. Then, once arrived at San Francisco, where he had friends of rank and position in the army, he would surely meet someone who knew her father well and possibly herself, some one to present him in due form, but for the present he could only hope to say a conventional word or two of gratitude, and he was striving to frame his thoughts as he hastened into the brightly lighted car and towards the section where last he had seen her.

It was occupied by a new-comer, a total stranger, and the three women recently sharing her section and more than sharing her cherries were now in animated chat across the aisle. In blank surprise and disappointment, Stuyvesant turned and sought the porter.

"Miss Ray! Yes, suh. She done got off at Sacramento, suh. Dere was friends come to meet her, and took her away in the carriage."

Once more Stuyvesant found himself constrained to seek the society of the maiden of uncertain years. Her presence was forbidding, her countenance severe, and her voice and intonation something appalling. But she might know Miss Ray's address; he could at least write his thanks; but he found the vice-president of the Order of the Patriotic Daughters of America in evil mood. She didn't know Miss Ray's address, and in the further assertion that she didn't want to know too readily betrayed the fact that her petulance was due to her not having been favored therewith.

"After all I did for her last night and to-day 'twould have been a mighty little thing to tell where she was going to stop, but just soon's her fine friends came aboard she dropped us like as if we weren't fit to notice."

The irate lady, however, seemed to find scant sympathy and support in the faces of her listeners, some of whom had long since wearied of her strident voice and oracular ways. It was well remembered that so far from being of aid or value in caring for the injured men, she had pestered people with undesired advice and interference, had made much noise and no bandages, and later, when an official of the company boarded the train, had constituted herself spokeswoman for the passengers, not at all to their advantage and much to his disgust. Then, finding that Miss Ray was looked upon as the only heroine of the occasion, she had assumed a guardian-ship, so to speak, over that young lady which became almost possessive in form, so passively was it tolerated.

She had plied the girl with questions as to the friends who were to meet her on arrival in San Francisco, and Miss Ray had smilingly given evasive answers.

When, therefore, they neared Sacramento and the vice-president announced her intention of sallying forth to see to it that proper victuals were provided for her soldier boys, Miss Ray had a few minutes in which to make her preparations, and the next thing the vice-president saw of her supposed ward and dependant, that young lady was in the embrace of a richly dressed and most distinguished looking woman, whose gray hair only served to heighten the refinement of her features. Just behind the elder lady stood a silk-hatted dignitary in the prime of life, and behind him a footman or valet, to whom the porter was handing Miss Ray's belongings.

And what the vice-president so much resented was that Miss Ray had not only never mentioned her purpose of leaving the train at Sacramento, but never so much as introduced her friends, at whom the vice-president smiled invitingly while accepting Miss Ray's courteous but brief thanks for "so much attention during the afternoon," but who merely bowed in acknowledgment when she would have addressed them on the subject of Miss Ray's being of so much help to her when help was so much needed, and who spirited the young lady away to the handsome carriage awaiting her.

The vice-president was distinctly of the opinion that folks didn't need to slink off in that way unless they were ashamed of where they were going or afraid of being found out, whereat Stuyvesant found himself gritting his teeth with wrath, and so whirled about and left her.

It was after midnight when they reached the pier at Oakland. There, under the great train-shed, track after track was covered with troop cars and a full regiment lay sleeping.

An alert young officer of the guard raised his hand in salute as Stuyvesant addressed him. No, there were no ambulances, no soldiers from the Presidio. They might be waiting across the ferry.

But how was he to get the injured men across the ferry, thought Stuyvesant. Two of them would have to be carried.

The long train, except that recruit car, was now emptied. The throng of passengers had gone on through the waiting-rooms and up the stairway to the saloon deck of the huge ferry-boat. If he purposed going, no time was to be lost, and the porter bearing his hand-luggage ventured a word to that effect.

Stuyvesant looked back. There were protruding heads at many of the windows of the recruit car, but, obedient to the instructions given by Connelly, no man, apparently, had left his place, and Connelly, though suffering, had evidently resumed control, much benefited by the services of another physician who had boarded the train in the late afternoon and renewed the bandages and dressings of the injured men. Then Stuyvesant became suddenly aware of a messenger-boy with a telegram. It was addressed to "Lieutenant Stuyvesant, A. D. C., Train No. 2, Oakland." Tearing it open, he read as follows:

"Report by wire condition of Recruit Foster. If serious, have him conveyed to St. Paul's Hospital. Commission as lieutenant and signal officer awaits him here."

It was signed by the adjutant-general at department head-quarters, San Francisco.

But the boy had still another. This too he held forth to Stuyvesant, and the latter, not noticing that it was addressed "Commanding Officer U. S. Troops, Train No. 2," mechanically opened and read and made a spring for the car.

The message was from Port Costa, barely thirty miles away, and briefly said: "Any your men missing? Soldier left car here believed jumped overboard return trip ferry-boat."

One man was missing. Recruit Foster, for whom a commission as lieutenant and signal officer was waiting at department head-quarters, could not be found.

CHAPTER IV

In the busy week that followed Lieutenant Stuyvesant had his full share of work and no time for social distraction. Appointed to the staff of General Vinton, with orders to sail without delay for Manila, the young officer found his hours from morn till late at night almost too short for the duties demanded of him.

The transports were almost ready. The troops had been designated for the expedition. The supplies were being hurried aboard. The general had his men all the livelong day at the rifle-ranges or drill-grounds, for most of the brigade were raw volunteers who had been rushed to the point of rendezvous with scant equipment and with less instruction. The camps were thronged with men in all manner of motley as to dress and no little variety as to dialect. Few of the newly appointed officers in the Department of Supply were versed in their duties, and the young regulars of the staff of the commanding general were working sixteen hours out of the twenty-four, coaching their comrades of the volunteers.

The streets were crowded with citizens eager to welcome and applaud the arriving troops. Hotels were thronged. Restaurants were doing a thriving business, for the army ration did not too soon commend itself in its simplicity to the stomachs of some thousands of young fellows who had known better diet if no better days, many of their number having left luxurious homes and surroundings and easy salaries to shoulder a musket for three dollars a week.

Private soldiers in blue flannel shirts were learning to stand attention and touch their caps to young men in shoulder-straps whom they had laughed at and called "tin soldiers" a year agone because they belonged to the militia—a thing most of the gilded youth in many of our Western cities seemed to scorn as beneath them.

In the wave of patriotic wrath and fervor that swept the land when the Maine was done to death in Havana Harbor, many and many a youth who has sneered at the State Guardsmen learned to wish that he too had given time and honest effort to the school of the soldier, for now, unless he had sufficient "pull" to win for him a staff position, his only hope was in the ranks.

And so, even in the recruit detachments of the regulars, were found scores of young men whose social status at home was on a plane much higher than that of many of their officers. But the time had come when the long and patient effort of the once despised militiaman had won deserved recognition. The commissions in the newly raised regiments were held almost exclusively by officers who had won them through long service with the National Guard.

And in the midst of all the whirl of work in which he found himself, Lieutenant Stuyvesant had been summoned to the tent of General Drayton, commanding the great encampment on the sand-lots south of the Presidio reservation, and bidden to tell what he knew of one Walter F. Foster, recruit—th Cavalry, member of the detachment sent on via the Denver and Rio Grande to Ogden, then transferred to the Southern Pacific train Number 2 *en route* to San Francisco, which detachment was burned out of its car and the car out of its train early on the morning of the—of June, 1898, somewhere in the neighborhood of a station with the uncouth name of Beowawe in the heart of the Humboldt Desert, and which Recruit Foster had totally disappeared the following evening, having been last seen by his comrades as the train was ferried across Carquinez Straits, thirty miles from Oakland Pier, and later by railway hands at Port Costa on the back trip of the big boat to the Benicia side.

There was little Stuyvesant could tell. He hardly remembered the man except as a fine-featured young fellow who seemed shy, nervous, and unstrung, something Stuyvesant had hitherto attributed to the startling and painful experience of the fire, and who, furthermore, seemed desirous of dodging the lieutenant, which circumstance Stuyvesant could not fathom at all, and if anything rather resented.

He explained to the general that he was in no wise responsible for the care of the detachment. He had only casually met them at Ogden, and circumstances later had thrown him into closer relation.

But the veteran general was desirous of further information. He sat at the pine table in his plainly furnished tent, looking thoughtfully into the frank and handsome face of the young officer, his fingers beating a tattoo on the table-top. The general's eyes were sombre, even sad at times. Beneath them lay lines of care and sorrow. His voice was low, his manner grave, courteous, even cold. He was studying his man and discussing in his mind how far he might confide in him.

Obedient to the general's invitation, Stuyvesant had taken a chair close to the commander's table and sat in silence awaiting further question. At last it came.

"You say he left nothing—no trace—behind?"

"There was nothing to leave, general. He had only a suit of underwear, in which he escaped from the car. The men say he had had money and a valise filled with things which he strove to keep from sight of any of his fellows. They say that he befriended a tough character by the name of Murray, who had enlisted with him, and they think Murray knows something about him."

"Where is Murray now?" asked the chief.

"In the guard-house at the Presidio. He gave the corporal in charge a good deal of trouble and was placed under guard the morning they reached the city. They had to spend the night with the Iowa regiment at Oakland Pier."

Again the gray-haired general gave himself to thought. "Could you tell how he was dressed when he disappeared?" he finally asked.

"A young man in the second sleeper gave him a pair of worn blue serge trousers and his morocco slippers. Somebody else contributed a *neglige* shirt and a black silk travelling cap. He was wearing these when last I spoke to him at Sacramento, where he would not eat anything. I—I had wired ahead for dinner for them."

"Yes," said the general with sudden indignation in his tone, "and I'm told the company refused to reimburse you. What excuse did they give?"

"It's of little consequence, sir," laughed Stuyvesant. "The loss hasn't swamped me."

"That's as may be," answered the general. "It's the principle involved. That company is coining money by the thousands transporting troops at full rates, and some of the cars it furnished were simply abominable. What was the excuse given?"

"They said, or rather some official wrote, that they wouldn't reimburse us because they had already had to sustain the loss of that car due to the carelessness of our men, and their own train-hands, general, knew there was no smoking and the men were all asleep. Foster had a very narrow escape, and Corporal Connelly was badly burned lugging Murray out."

The general took from a stack of correspondence at his right hand a letter on club paper, studied it a moment, and then glanced up at Stuyvesant. "Was not Colonel Ray's regiment with you at Chickamauga?" he asked.

"It was expected when I left, general. You mean the—th Kentucky?"

"I mean his volunteer regiment—yes. I was wondering whether any of his family had gone thither. But you wouldn't be apt to know."

And Stuyvesant felt the blood beginning to mount to his face. He could answer for it that one member had not gone thither. He was wondering whether he ought to speak of it when Drayton finally turned upon him and held forth the letter. "Read that," said he, "but regard it as confidential."

It was such a letter as one frank old soldier might write another. It was one of a dozen that had come to Drayton that day asking his interest in behalf of some young soldier about joining his command. It was dated at Cincinnati five days earlier, and before Stuyvesant had read half through the page his hand was trembling.

"Dear Drayton," it said, "I'm in a snarl, and I want your help. My sister's pet boy came out to try his hand at ranching near us last year. He had some money from his father and everything promised well for his success if he could have stuck to business. But he couldn't. Billy Ray, commanding my first squadron, was stationed with me, and the first thing I knew the boy was head over ears in love with Billy's daughter. I can't blame him. Marion, junior, is as pretty a girl as ever grew up in the army, and she's a brave and winsome lass besides—her Dad all over, as her mother says.

"Walter's ranch was thirty miles away, but he'd ride the sixty six times a week, if need be, to have a dance with Maidie Ray, and the cattle could go to the wolves. Then came the war. The Governor of Kentucky gave Ray the command of a regiment, and that fool boy of mine begged him to take him along. Ray couldn't. Besides, I don't think he half liked Walter's devotions to the girl, though he hadn't anything against him exactly. Then I was retired and sent home, and the next thing my sister, Mrs. Foster, came tearing in to tell me Walter had gone and enlisted—enlisted in the regulars at Denver and was going to 'Frisco and Manila, as he couldn't get to Cuba. She's completely broke up about it.

"Foster went to Washington and saw the President and got a commission for him in the signal corps,—volunteers,—and he should be with you by the time you get this, so I wired ahead.

"He isn't altogether a bad lot, but lacks horse sense, and gave his parents a good deal of anxiety in his varsity days abroad. He was in several scrapes along with a boon companion who seems to have been so much like him, physically and morally, that, mother-like, Mrs. Foster is sure that very much of which her Walter was accused was really done by Wally's chum. I'm not so sure of this myself, but at all events Foster made it a condition that the boy should cut loose from the evil association, as he called it, before certain debts would be paid. I don't know what soldier stuff there is in him—if any—but give him a fair start for old times' sake.

"I need not tell you that I wish you all the joy and success the double stars can bring. I'd be in it too but for that old Spotsylvania shot-hole and rheumatics. My eagles, however, will fold their wings and take a rest, but we'll flap 'em and scream every time you make a ten-strike.

"Yours, as ever,

"Martindale."

Stuyvesant did not look up at once after finishing the letter. When he did, and before he could speak, the general was holding out some telegrams, and these too he took and read—the almost agonized appeals of a mother for news of her boy—the anxious inquiries, coupled with suggestions of the veteran soldier concerning the only son of a beloved sister. Drayton's fine, thoughtful face was full of sympathy— his eyes clouded with anxiety and sorrow. Martindale was not the only old soldier in search of son or nephew that fateful summer.

"You see how hard it is to be able to send no tidings whatever," he said. "I sent to you in the hope that you might think of some possible explanation, might suggest some clue or theory. Can you?"

There was just one moment of silence, and then again Stuyvesant looked up, his blue eyes meeting the anxious gaze of the commander.

"General," he hazarded, "it is worth while to try Sacramento. Miss Ray is there."

CHAPTER V

At sunset that evening the regiments destined to embark with the expedition commanded by General Vinton were paraded for inspection in full marching order, while a dozen other commands less fortunate looked enviously on. The day had been raw and chilly. The wind blew salt and strong, sending the fog in dripping clouds sailing in at the Golden Gate, obscuring all the bold northern shore, and streaming up the sandy slopes and over the wide wastes south of Sutro Heights. Men who owned overcoats were few and far between, so while the designated battalions stood and shivered in the wet grass, the mass of spectators hovered about in ponchos or wrapped in blankets, the down-turned brims of their campaign hats dripping heavily and contributing much to the weird and unmilitary look of the wearers. Officers had donned Mackintoshes and heavy boots. Badges of rank, except in cases of those provided with the regulation overcoat, were lost to sight. Only among the regulars and one or two regiments made up from the National Guard were uniforms so complete that in their foul-weather garb it was possible to distinguish colonel from subaltern, staff sergeant from private.

In front of the guard-house at the Presidio a dozen cavalry-men armed with the new carbine and dressed throughout for winter service, this being San Francisco June, had formed ranks under command of a sergeant and stood silently at ease awaiting the coming of the officer of the day. The accurate fit of their warm overcoats, the cut of their trooper trousers, the polish of their brasses and buttons, the snug, trim "set" of their belts, all combined to tell the skilled observer that these were regulars.

As such they were objects of interest and close scrutiny to the little knots of volunteers who had sauntered in to pick up points. To the former it looked odd and out of gear to see the forage-caps and broad white stripes of commissioned officers mingling with the slouch hats and ill-fitting nether garments of the rank and file.

It was too early in the campaign for "the boys" to have settled down to realization of the subtle distinction between their status as soldiers of the Nation and citizens of a sovereign State. To private A of the far Westerners his company commander was still "Billy, old boy," or at best "Cap.," save when actually in ranks and on drill or parade.

To the silently observant volunteer, on the other hand, it was just as odd to note that when a gray-haired veteran sergeant, issuing from the guard-house, caught sight of a trig, alert little fellow, with beardless face and boyish features and keen, snapping dark eyes, hastening towards him in the garb of a lieutenant of cavalry, the veteran was suddenly transformed into a rigid statue in light blue, standing attention and at the salute—a phenomenon that extracted from the infant officer only a perfunctory touch of finger to cap visor and not so much as a glance.

How could the "boys" from far Nebraska be supposed to know that the little chap had spent his whole life in the shadow of the flag, and had many a time in baby days been dandled on the very arm that was now so deferentially bent and uplifted in soldier homage? What was there in the manner of the youngster to betray the fact that he dreaded old Sergeant Rigney's criticism even more than that of his commanding officer?

Then came another phenomenon.

At a brief, curt "Sergeant, get out your prisoners," from the beardless lips, there was instant fumbling of big keys and clanking of iron from the hidden recesses of the guard-house.

The dismounted troopers sprang suddenly to attention. The guard split in two at its middle, each half facing outward, marched half a dozen paces away like the duellists of old days from the back to back position, halted, faced front once more, and stood again at ease, with a broad gap of a dozen paces between their inner flanks.

Into this space, shuffling dejectedly in some cases, stalking defiantly in others, slinking, shivering, and decrepit in the case of two or three poor wrecks of the rum fiend, a stream of humanity in soiled soldier garb came pouring from the prison door and lined up under the eyes of vigilant non-commissioned officers in front of the young lieutenant in command.

There they stood, their eyes shifting nervously from group to group of huddling spectators, their shoulders hunched up to their ears—the riff-raff of the garrison—the few desperate, dangerous characters from the surrounding camps, an uncouth, uncanny lot at any time, but looking its worst in the drip of the floating fog-wreaths and the gloom and despond of the dying day. The boom of the sunset gun from Alcatraz fell sullenly on the ear even as the soft trumpets of the cavalry, close at hand, began sounding the "Retreat." At its last prolonged note the sharp crack of an old three-inch rifle

Charles King

echoed the report from Alcatraz, and from the invisible, mist-shrouded top of the staff the dripping folds of the storm-flag came flapping down in view, limp and bedraggled, and the guard sprang again to attention as a burly, red-faced, hearty-looking soldier, with a captain's insignia in loop and braid on the sleeves of his overcoat, broke a way through the group of lookers-on and, barely waiting for the salute and report of the young lieutenant commanding, began a sharp scrutiny of the prisoners before him.

Down along the line he went, until at the fourth man from the left in the front rank he stopped short. A bulky, thick-set soldier stood there, a sullen, semi-defiant look about his eyes, a grim set to the jaws bristling with a week-old beard of dirty black. Then came the snapping colloquy.

"Your name Murray?"

"That's what they call me."

"What was your name before that?"

"Jim."

Whereat there was a titter in the ranks of prisoners. Some of the guard even allowed their mouths to expand, and the groups of volunteers, chuckling in keen enjoyment, came edging in closer.

Instantly the voice of the officer of the guard was heard ordering silence, and faces straightened out in the twinkling of an eye.

The elder officer, the captain, grew a trifle redder, but he was master of himself and the situation. It is with school-boys as with soldiers, their master is the man whom pranks or impudence cannot annoy. The officer of the day let no tone of temper into his next question. Looking straight into the shifting eyes, he waited for perfect silence, and then spoke:

"Jim what? I wish the name under which you served in your previous enlistment."

"Never said I'd served before."

"No. You declared you had not. But I know better. You're a deserter from the Seventh Cavalry."

The face under the shrouding campaign hat went gray white with sudden twitch of the muscles, then set again, rigid and defiant. The eyes snapped angrily. The answer was sharp, yet seemed, as soldiers say, to "hang fire" a second.

"Never seen the Seventh Cavalry in my life."

The officer of the day turned and beckoned to a figure hitherto kept well in the background, screened by the groups of surrounding volunteers. A man of middle age, smooth shaven and stout, dressed in business sack-suit, came sturdily forward and took position by the captain's side.

At sight of the new-comer Murray's face, that had regained a bit of its ruddy hue, again turned dirty white, and the boy lieutenant, eying him closely, saw the twitch of his thin, half-hidden lips.

"Point out your man," said the captain to the new arrival.

The civilian stepped forward, and without a word twice tapped with his forefinger the broad breast of Prisoner Murray and, never looking at him, turned again to the officer of the day.

"What was his name in the Seventh?" asked the latter.

"Sackett."

The captain turned to the officer of the guard. "Mr. Ray," said he, "separate Murray from the garrison prisoners and have him put in a cell. That man must be carefully guarded. You may dismiss the guard, sir."

And, followed by the stranger, Captain Kress was leaving the ground when Murray seemed to recover himself, and in loud and defiant voice gave tongue,—

"That man's a damned liar, and this is an outrage."

"Shut up, Murray!" shouted the sergeant of the guard, scandalized at such violation of military proprieties. "It's gagged you'll be, you idiot," he added between his set teeth, as with scowling face he bore down on the equally scowling prisoner. "Come out of that and step along here ahead of me. I'll put you where shoutin' won't help." And slowly, sullenly, Murray obeyed.

Slowly and in silence the groups of spectators broke up and sauntered away as the last of the prisoners dragged back into the guard-house, and the guard itself broke ranks and went within doors, leaving only the sentry pacing mechanically the narrow, hard-beaten path, the sergeant, and at the turn of the road, the young lieutenant whom Captain Kress had addressed as Mr. Ray. This officer, having silently received his superior's orders and seen to it that Murray was actually "behind the bars," had again come forth into the gathering twilight, the gloaming of a cheerless day, and having hastened to the bend from which point the forms of the officer of the day and his associate were still faintly visible, stood gazing after them, a puzzled look in his brave young face.

Not yet a month in possession of his commission, here was a lad to whom every iota of the routine of a lieutenant's life was as familiar as though he had drawn the pay for a decade.

Born and bred in the army, taught from early boyhood to ride and shoot, to spar and swim, spending his vacation in saddle and his schooldays in unwilling study, an adept in every healthful and exhilarating sport, keen with rifle and revolver, with shotgun and rod, with bat and racquet, with the gloves and Indian clubs, the nimblest quarter-back and dodger, the swiftest runner of his school, it must be owned that Mr. Sanford Ray was a most indifferent scholar. Of geography, history, and languages he had rather more than a smattering because of occasional tours abroad when still at an impressionable age. Yet Sandy "took more stock," as he expressed it, and "stawk," as he called it, in Sioux and the sign language than he did in French or German, knew far more of the Rockies and Sierras than he did of the Alps, studied the European cavalry with the eye of an accomplished critic, and stoutly maintained that while they were bigger swells and prettier to look at, they could neither ride nor shoot to compare with the sturdy troopers of his father's squadron.

"As to uniforms," said Sandy, "anybody could look swagger in the lancer and huzzar rig. It takes a man to look like a soldier in what our fellows have to wear."

It wasn't the field garb Sandy despised, but the full dress, the blue and yellow enormity in which our troopers are compelled to appear.

It had been the faint hope of his fond parents that Master Sandy would grow up to be something, by which was meant a lawyer, an artist, architect, engineer,—something in civil life that promised home and fortune. But the lad from babyhood would think of nothing but the army and with much misgiving, in Sandy's fifteenth year, his father shipped him to Kentucky, where they were less at home than in Kansas, and gave him a year's hard schooling in hopes of bracing up his mathematics.

Sandy was wild to go to West Point, and at the bottom of his heart Major Ray would have rejoiced had he thought it possible for Sandy to pull through; but ruefully he minded him how hard a task was his own, and how close he came to failure at the semi-annual exams. "Sandy hates Math. even more than I did," said he to Marion, his devoted wife. "It was all I could do to squirm through when the course was nowhere near as hard as it is to-day, so don't set your heart on it, little woman."

The appointment was not so hard to get, for Major Billy had a host of friends in his native State, and an old chum at the Point assured him he could coach young Sandy through the preliminary, and indeed he did. Sandy scraped in after six months' vigorous work, managed to hold his own through the first year's tussle with algebra and geometry, which he had studied hard and faithfully before, was a pet in his class, and the pride and joy of his mother's and sister's heart in yearling camp, where he blossomed out in corporal's chevrons and made as natty and active a first sergeant as could be found while the "furlough class" was away.

But the misery began with "analytical" and the crisis came with calculus, and to the boy's bitter sorrow, after having been turned back one year on the former and failing utterly on the latter, the verdict of the Academic Board went dead against him, and stout old soldiers thereon cast their votes with grieving hearts, for "Billy Ray's Boy" was a lad they hated to let go, but West Point rules are inexorable.

So too were there saddened hearts far out on the frontier where the major was commanding a cavalry post in a busy summer, but neither he nor Marion had one word of blame or reproach for the boy. Loving arms, and eyes that smiled through their sorrow, welcomed him when the little chap returned to them. "Don't anybody come to meet me," he wrote. "Just let mother be home." And so it was settled.

He sprang from the wagon that met him at the station, went hand in hand with his father into the hall, and then, with one sob, bounded into Marion's outstretched arms as she stood awaiting him in the little army parlor.

The major softly closed the door and with blinking eyes stole away to stables. There had been another meeting a little later when Marion the second was admitted, and the girl stole silently to her brother's side and her arms twined about his neck. Her love for him had been something like adoration through all the years of girlhood, and now, though he was twenty and she eighteen, its fervor seemed to know no diminution. They had done their best, all of them, to encourage while the struggle lasted, but to teach him that should failure come, it would come without reproach or shame.

The path to success in other fields was still before him. The road to the blessed refuge of home and love and sympathy would never close.

It was hard to reconcile the lad at first. The major set him up as a young ranchman in a lovely valley in the Big Horn Range, and there he went sturdily to work, but before the winter was fairly on the country was rousing to the appeals of Cuba, and before it was gone the Maine had sunk, a riddled hulk, and the spring came in with a call to arms.

Together with some two hundred young fellows all over the land, Sanford Ray went up for examination for the vacant second lieutenancies in the army, and he who had failed in analytical and calculus passed without grave trouble the more practical ordeal demanded by the War Department, was speedily commissioned in the artillery, and, to his glory and delight, promptly transferred to the cavalry.

Then came the first general break up the family had really known, for the major hurried away to Kentucky to assume command of the regiment of volunteers of which he had been made colonel. Billy, junior, a lad of barely seventeen, enlisted at Lexington as a bugler in his father's regiment, and swore he'd shoot himself if they didn't let him serve. The Kentuckians were ordered to Chickamauga, the young regular to the Presidio at San Francisco, and Mrs. Ray, after seeing her husband and youngest son started for the South, returned to Leavenworth, where they had just settled down a week before the war began, packed and stored the household furniture, then, taking "Maidie" with her, hurried westward to see the last of her boy, whose squadron was destined for service at Manila.

The lieutenant, as they delighted in calling him, joined them at Denver, looking perfectly at home in his field uniform and perfectly happy. They left Maidie to spend a week with old army friends at Fort Douglas, and as soon as Sandy was settled in his new duties and the loving mother had satisfied herself the cavalry would not be spirited away before July, she accepted the eager invitation of other old friends to visit them at Sacramento, and there they were, mother and daughter, again united this very raw and foggy evening, when Mr. Ray, as officer of the guard, stood at the bend of the roadway east of the Presidio guard-house, gazing after the vanishing forms of Captain Kress and the burly stranger in civilian clothes, and wondering where on earth it was he had seen the latter before.

So engrossed was he in this that it was only when a second time addressed that he whirled about and found himself confronting a tall and slender young officer, with frank, handsome blue eyes and fine, clear-cut face, a man perhaps five years his senior in age and one grade in rank, for his overcoat sleeve bore the single loop and braid of a first lieutenant.

He was in riding boots and spurs, as Ray noted at first glance, and there behind him stood an orderly holding the horses of both.

"Pardon me. I am Lieutenant Stuyvesant of General Vinton's staff. This is the officer of the guard, I believe, and I am sent to make some inquiry of a prisoner—a man named Murray."

"We have such a man," said Ray, eying the newcomer with soldierly appreciation of his general appearance and not without envy of his inches. "But he's just been locked in a cell, and it will take an order from the officer of the day to fetch him out—unless you could see him in there with other prisoners within earshot."

"Not very well," answered Stuyvesant, looking curiously into the dark eyes of the youngster. "Perhaps I'd better see the officer of the day at once."

"You'll find him at the club. He's just gone in," said Ray, mindful of the fact that this was the captain's time for a cocktail, and with a courteous salute the aide-de-camp hastened away.

In five minutes he was back with a pencilled scrawl from Kress to the effect that Lieutenant Stuyvesant was to be permitted to interview the prisoner Murray outside the guard-house, but sentries must be placed to prevent escape.

Quickly young Ray called out the corporal and two men, warned them of the duty demanded, stationed them up and down the road and opposite the guard-house, but just out of ear-shot, ordered the prisoner brought forth, and then, leaving Stuyvesant standing at the post of Number One, stepped a dozen yards away into the mist.

A minute later out came the sergeant, marshalling Murray after him, a sentry at his heels. Then in the gathering darkness the tall officer and the short, thick-set soldier met face to face, and the latter recoiled and began glancing quickly, furtively about him.

Just how it all happened Ray could never quite tell. The light was now feeble, the lamps were only just beginning to burn. There was a moment of low-toned talk between the two, a question twice repeated in firmer tone, then a sudden, desperate spring and dash for liberty.

Like a centre rush—a charging bull—the prisoner came head on straight to where young Ray was standing, heedless of a yell to halt, and in less time than it takes to tell it, the lithe little athlete of West Point's crack football team had sprung and tackled and downed him in his tracks.

Biting, cursing, straining, the big bully lay in the mud, overpowered now by the instant dash of the guard, while their bantam officer, rising and disgustedly contemplating the smear of wet soil over his new overcoat, was presently aware of Stuyvesant, bending forward, extending a helping hand, and exclaiming:

"By Jove, but that was a neat tackle! You must have been a

joy to *your* team. What was it?"

"West Point—last year's."

"And may I ask—the name?"

"My name's Ray," said Sandy with beaming smile, showing a row of even, white teeth under the budding, dark mustache, and Stuyvesant felt the warm blood surging to his forehead, just as it had before that day in the general's tent.

"I think I should have known that," he presently stammered. "It was Miss Ray who so skilfully treated those poor fellows burned out on our train. I suppose you heard of it."

"Why, yes," answered the youngster, again curiously studying the face of his tall visitor. "Then it was you she—I heard about. Wish I weren't on duty. I'd be glad to have you over at my quarters or the club."

"I wish so too, and yet I'm lucky in finding you here, since"—and here Stuyvesant turned and looked resentfully towards the bedraggled figure of Murray, now being supported back to the cells—"since that fellow proved so churlish and ungrateful. He's all wrath at being put behind the bars and won't answer any questions."

"What else could he expect?" asked Ray bluntly. "He's a deserter."

"A deserter!" exclaimed Stuyvesant in surprise. "Who says so?"

"Captain Kress, officer of the day, or at least a cit who came with him to identify him. They say he skipped from the Seventh Cavalry."

At this piece of information Mr. Stuyvesant whirled about again in added astonishment. "Why," said he, "this upsets—one theory completely. I declare, if that's true we're all at sea. I beg pardon," he continued, but now with marked hesitancy—"you know—you've heard, I suppose, about—Foster?"

"What Foster?"

"Why, the recruit, you know, the one we lost at Port Costa," and the blue eyes were curiously and intently studying the face of the younger soldier, dimly visible now that the guard-house lamps were beginning to glow.

"I knew there was a recruit missing, and—seems to me that was the name," answered Ray.

"And—didn't you know who he was—that it was—pardon me, the man who—lived near you—had a ranch—"

"Great Scott! You don't mean Wally Foster! *He* enlisted and in the cavalry? Well, I'm—" And now Mr. Ray's merriment overcame him. "I never thought there was that much to Wally. He was a lackadaisical sort of a spook when I saw him. What possessed him to enlist? He's no stuff for a soldier."

Stuyvesant hesitated. That letter of old Colonel Martindale's was shown him in confidence. But Ray's next impetuous outburst settled it.

"Oh, by Jove! I see it,—it's—" And here the white teeth gleamed in the lamplight, for Mr. Ray was laughing heartily.

"Yes? It's what?" smiled Stuyvesant sympathetically.

"It's—my sister, I reckon," laughed Ray. "She once said she wouldn't marry outside of the army, and he heard it."

"Oh,—did she?" said Stuyvesant reflectively, and then he was silent.

CHAPTER VI

When Vinton's flotilla drew out into that wonderful bay, and the crowded transports rode at anchor on the tide, there came swarming about them all manner of harbor craft, some laden with comforts for the departing soldiery, some with curiosity seekers, some with contraband of war in the shape of fruit and fluids, but all were warned to keep a cable's length at least away.

The commanding general, with other officers of rank, was darting from ship to ship in a swift steam launch, holding brief conference with the colonel in command of each, and finally repairing to his own—the flagship—where the final adieux were exchanged.

The general and his aides nimbly mounted the steep stairway to the bridge, the launch swung loose, and then up to the mast-head flew a little bunch of bunting that broke as it reached the truck, and there fluttered in the strong salt wind whistling in from sea the eagerly awaited signal to "up anchor and follow."

And then at the stern of the Vanguard the waves were churned into foam as the massive screw began its spin, and slowly, steadily the flagship forged ahead to the accompaniment of a deafening din of steam whistles and sirens all over the bay. Promptly the other transports followed the movements of the leader, and presently, in trailing column, five big black steamships, thronged with cheering soldiery, were slowly ploughing their way towards the grand entrance of that spacious harbor, the matchless Golden Gate.

Coming abreast of rock-ribbed Alcatraz, still moving at less than half speed, the flagship was greeted by the thunder of the parting salute, and the commanding general, standing with his staff upon the bridge, doffed his cap and bared his handsome head in acknowledgment.

"The next guns we're apt to hear will be the Spaniard's at Manila, and shotted guns instead of blanks," said a staff officer to the tall, fair-haired aide-de-camp. "What's the matter, Stuyvesant? Beginning to feel wabbly already? There's no sea here to speak of."

"I was watching that boat," was the quiet reply, as the young officer pointed to a small white steamer that appeared coming in pursuit, carefully picking a way through the host of harbor craft still screeching and steaming along as escort to the fleet.

There was an eager light in the bright blue eyes, but the high color had fled. Stuyvesant looked as though he had not slept as much or as well of late as perfect health required, and his questioner gazed keenly into his face, then turned away with a smile.

Only three days before, on the register of the Occidental appeared among the arrivals the entry "Mrs. William P. Ray, Miss Ray, Fort Leavenworth," and that evening at least a dozen officers called and sent up their cards, and Lieutenant Ray came in from the Presidio and was with his mother and sister an hour or more.

The ladies held quite a little levee in the parlor of the familiar old army hostelry, and Mr. Stuyvesant, after a long and fatiguing day's duty at camp, accompanied his general to their very handsome apartments at The Palace, and then falteringly asked if he might be excused awhile—he had a call or two to make.

The evening papers had announced the arrival of the wife and daughter of "the gallant officer so well known for quarter of a century gone by to many of our citizens—Captain 'Billy' Ray, now colonel of the—th Kentucky," and Stuyvesant had determined to make an effort to meet them. But he was a stranger to the officers who called and sent up their cards—all old regulars.

Lieutenant Ray was with the party in the parlor, and Stuyvesant felt a strange shyness when striving to persuade himself to send his card to that young officer and boldly ask to be presented. Surely it was the proper thing to seek and meet her and thank her for her deft ministrations the night of the fire. Surely a man of his distinguished family and connections need not shrink from asking to be introduced to any household in all our broad domain, and yet Stuyvesant found himself nervous and hesitant, wandering about the crowded office, making pretense of interest in posters and pictures, wistfully regarding the jovial knots of regulars who seemed so thoroughly at home.

Over at The Palace, where so many of the general officers and their staffs were quartered, he had dozens of friends. Here at this favorite old resort of the regular service he stood alone, and to his proud and sensitive spirit it seemed as though there were a barrier between him and these professional soldiers.

There was the whole secret of his trouble. Absurd and trivial as it may seem, Stuyvesant shrank from the enterprise, even at the very threshold,—shrank even from sending his card and asking for Lieutenant Ray, for no other or better reason than that he did not know how a volunteer would be welcomed.

And so for nearly half an hour he hovered irresolute about the office, unconscious of the many glances of interest and admiration from the keen eyes of the officers gathered in laughing groups about the marbled floor. Not one of their number was his superior in form and feature, and his uniform was the handiwork of Gotham's best military tailor. *They* saw that the instant he threw off his cape.

One of their number whispered that it was Mr. Stuyvesant, General Vinton's aide, for everybody knew Vinton, and more than one would have been glad to take the aide-de-camp by the hand and bid him welcome to their coterie but for that same odd shyness that, once away from camp or garrison and in the atmosphere of metropolitan life, seems to clog and hamper the kindlier impulses of the soldier.

Presently, as Stuyvesant stood at the desk looking over the register, he heard himself accosted by name, and turning quickly, hopefully, found to his disappointment only a stocky little man in civilian dress. Yet the face was familiar, and the trouble in the honest brown eyes looking up to him, as though for help and sympathy, went right to his heart. Even before the man could give his name or tell his need, Stuyvesant knew him and held out a cordial hand:

"Why! You're our brakeman! I'm glad to see you. What's wrong?"

"I've lost me job, sir," was the answer, with a little choke. "They let me out two days ago—for sayin' their rotten old car caught fire from the boxes, I reckon."

"You don't tell me!" exclaimed Stuyvesant in honest indignation. "Now, how can I help you? What shall we do?"

"Take me to Manila, sir. I don't need this place. There's no one dependent on me—I can't soldier. They won't 'list a fellow with only two fingers," and he held up a maimed hand. "Lost the others in a freight smash-up six years ago. But there's a railway out there that'll be ours in a few months. Then you'll want Yankee train-hands. Can you do that much for me, lieutenant?"

"Come to me at The Palace at eight o'clock in the morning," answered Stuyvesant. "I'll have had a chance to talk to my general by that time. Meanwhile"—and with a blush he began drawing forth his purse.

The brakeman smiled. "I've got money enough, sir. They paid me off and I had some put by. Thank you all the same, Mr. Stuyvesant.—Oh, yes, sir, I'm ready," he broke off suddenly in addressing some other person, and Stuyvesant, turning quickly to see, was confronted by Lieutenant Ray.

"Oh, how-de-do? Going to be here long?" promptly queried that young gentleman. "Haven't seen you since the night at the Presidio. 'Scuse me, will you, I've got to take—er—my sister wants to see the brakeman, you know.—With you the night of the fire." And with that Mr. Ray hopped briskly away to the elevator, the ex-trainman following, leaving Stuyvesant standing enviously at the counter.

Even a brakeman could go to her and hear her pleasant words and receive that beaming smile and perhaps a clasp of that cool, slender little hand, while he who so longed for it all stood without the pale.

Then an impulse that had been spurring him for half an hour overmastered him. The parlors were public. At least he could go and take a peep at her.

He started for the elevator, then changed his plan, turned, and, with his cape still thrown over his arm, ascended the stairs. The clerk at the office desk glanced curiously at him, but the uniform was sufficient. In a moment he found himself in the broad corridor and almost in front of the doorway to the parlor. Half a dozen groups, women and officers, were scattered about in merry conversation, but Stuyvesant's eyes were riveted instantly on a little party close by the elevator shaft. There, hat in hand, bowing and blushing, stood the brakeman. There, with a bright, genial smile on her serene and happy face, stood a matronly woman who, despite her soft blue eyes and fair hair and complexion, was patent at once as the mother of the lovely, dark-eyed girl and the trim young soldier who formed the other members of the group.

Three or four officers, some of them past the meridian, others young subalterns, stood looking on in evident interest, and Stuyvesant halted spellbound, not knowing just what to do.

It was over in a moment. The railwayman, confused but happy, had evidently been the recipient of kind and appreciative words, for his face was glowing, and Miss Ray's fairly beamed with the radiance of its smile. Then the door flew open as the elevator-car stopped for passengers, and the ex-brakeman backed in and disappeared from view. Then the mother twined an arm about her daughter's slender waist and two young officers sprang forward to her side. Together they came sauntering towards the parlor door, and then, all on a sudden, she looked up and saw him.

There was no mistaking the flash of instant recognition in her beautiful eyes. Stuyvesant's heart leaped as his eager

Charles King

gaze met the swift glance, and noted with joy that she certainly saw and knew him: more than that, that the sight gave her pleasure. But in another instant she had recovered herself, and turned to ask some quick question of the young gallant at her side, and Stuyvesant, who was almost at the point of bowing low, found himself savagely hating those yellow straps and stripes and wishing the cavalry in perdition. Somebody was speaking to Mr. Ray, and he couldn't catch that young officer's eye. The party stopped a moment at the threshold, one of the officers was saying good-night, and then a voice at Stuyvesant's elbow said "Which is Lieutenant Ray?" It was the bell-boy.

A sudden inspiration came to Stuyvesant. "What is it?" he said. "Have you a message for him?"

"Yes," was the answer. "They're telephoning for him from the Presidio,—want him to come at once."

"Tell me the whole message and I'll give it," said Stuyvesant. "Anything wrong?"

"Yes, sir. The clerk's at the 'phone now, but I couldn't get the trouble. Something's broke loose, as I understand it."

And that delay was fatal. Bounding up the steps, three at a stride, came a young officer, breathless, and made straight for the group. Seeing that Mrs. Ray and Miss Marion were close at hand, he paused one moment, then with significant gesture called Ray to his side. Then Stuyvesant could not but hear every word of the sudden and startling message.

"Ray, you're wanted at the barracks at once. Prisoners 'scaped and your house is robbed!"

Stuyvesant ran beside him as Ray went bounding down the

stairs and out into Montgomery Street.

"Can I be of any service? Can I help you some way?" he urged, for he saw the young officer was looking white and anxious. But Ray hurriedly thanked him and declined. He could not imagine, he said, what his loss might be, yet something told him if anybody had escaped it was that hulking sinner Murray.

He sprang upon the first street-car at the corner, waved his hand in parting, and was whisked away westward, leaving Stuyvesant standing disconsolate.

How now could he hope to meet her? The clerk at the office seemed friendly and sympathetic when Stuyvesant wandered back there, and gave him such particulars of the situation at the Presidio as he had been able to gather over the wire. It seemed that a rumor had reached the commanding officer that a number of tools had been smuggled into the guard-house by the prisoners, and by the aid of these they hoped to cut their way out. Despite the fact that it was growing dark, a search of the prison room and cells was ordered while the prisoners stood in line in front awaiting the usual evening inspection. There was no one to tell just who started it or how, but, all on a sudden, while many of the guard were aiding in the search inside, the whole array of prisoners, regular and volunteer, old and young, except those few in irons, made a sudden and simultaneous dash for liberty, scattering in every direction. Some had already been recaptured, but at least twenty-five were still at large, and the post adjutant, telephoning for Ray, briefly added that there was every evidence that his quarters had been robbed.

All this Stuyvesant heard with an absorbing interest, wondering whether it might not be possible to make it a plea or pretext on which to present himself to Mrs. Ray, and then ask to be presented to her daughter. A second time he ascended the stairs and, sauntering by, peered in at the parlor-door. Yes, there sat the charming matron looking so winsome and kind as she smiled upon her circle of visitors, but, alas, they were four in number and all officers of rank in the regular service, and Stuyvesant's shyness again overcame him.

Moreover, his brief glance into the brightly lighted apartment, all decorated as it was with flags and flowers, revealed Miss Ray seated near the window with two young cavalrymen in devoted attendance—all three apparently so absorbed in their chat that he, lonely and wistful, escaped observation entirely until, just as he passed from view, her lovely dark eyes were for an instant quickly raised, and though he knew it not, she saw him, and saw too that he was wandering aimlessly about, but, quick as woman's intuition, her eyes returned to the face of the eager young trooper by her side, for Stuyvesant turned for one more longing glance before descending, defeated, to the office floor.

It was his last opportunity, and fate seemed utterly against him, for when on the following evening his general went to call upon Mrs. Ray and took his handsome and hopeful aide, "The ladies are out," said the bell-boy. They were dining at the adjutant-general's.

In desperation, Stuyvesant went over to a florist's on Post Street, bought a box of superb roses, and sent them with his card to Miss Ray, expressing deep regret that he had been denied opportunity to thank her in person for her kindness to him the night of the fire. He wanted to say that he owed his eyes to her, but felt that she knew better and would be more offended than pleased.

He was to sail on the morrow, and he had not even seen her brother again.

But the department commander had said he purposed coming out with a party of friends to run alongside the flag-ship as she steamed slowly out to sea, and that was why Mr. Stuyvesant stood so eagerly watching the ploughing side-wheeler so swiftly coming in pursuit. Already he had made out the double stars in the bunting at the jack-staff. Already he could distinguish the forms of several general officers whose commands were not yet ready for embarkation and the fluttering garments of a score of women.

Something told him she would be of the party, and as the Vanguard slowed down to let the head-quarters' boat run alongside, his heart beat eagerly when his general said: "We'll go down, gentlemen, and board her. It'll be much easier than the climb would be to them."

So it happened that five minutes later he found himself at the heels of his chief shaking hands mechanically with a dozen officers, while his eyes kept peering beyond them to where, on the after-deck, the smiling group of women stood expectant.

And presently the general pushed on for a word of farewell with them, the aides obediently following, and then came more presentations to cordial and kindly people whose names he did not even hear, for just a little farther on, and still surrounded by cavaliers, stood Mrs. Ray, the handsomest and most distinguished-looking woman of the party, and close beside her, *petite* and graceful, her dark beauty even the more noticeable in contrast with the fair features of her mother, stood Maidie. And then at last it came, the simple words that threw down the social barrier that so long had balked him.

"My aide-de-camp, Mr. Stuyvesant, Mrs. Ray,—Miss Ray," and with his soul in his eyes he looked down into that radiant face, smiling so cordially, unconstrainedly into his, and then found himself striving to recall what on earth it was he was so anxious to say.

He knew that he was flushing to the peak of his forage-cap. He knew he was trying to stammer something. He saw that she was perfectly placid and at her ease. He saw, worse luck, that she wore a little knot of roses on the breast of her natty jacket, but that they were not his. He faltered something to the effect that he had been trying to see her ever since the night of the fire—had so much to thank her for; and her white, even, beautiful teeth gleamed as she laughingly answered that the cherries had more than cancelled the score.

He asked for news of her brother, and was told that he had been too much occupied to come in again. They were going out to the Presidio that afternoon.

And then he ventured to hope Mr. Ray had sustained no great loss in the robbery of his quarters, and saw at once that he was breaking news, for the smile vanished instantly, the lovely face clouded with concern, and he had only time to stammer: "Then, probably, there was no truth in the story. I merely happened to hear two nights ago that Mr. Ray's quarters had been robbed,—about the time the prisoners escaped." And then he heard his general calling, and saw that the party was already clambering back to the Vanguard.

"I—I—I hope I may see you when we get back from Manila, Miss Ray," he said, as he bowed over her hand.

"I think you may see me—before that," was the smiling answer. And then Captain Hawley grabbed him by the arm and rushed him to the side.

Two minutes more and he was on the deck of the transport.

The lines were cast off, the white side-wheeler, alive with sympathetic faces, some smiling, some tearful, and a forest of fluttering kerchiefs, dropped slowly astern, and all that long evening as they bored through the fogs of the Farallones and bowed and dipped to the long swell of the sea, and all the long week that followed as they steamed over a sunlit summer ocean, Stuyvesant found himself repeating again and again her parting words, and wondering what could have been the explanation of her knowing nothing of the robbery of her brother's quarters, or what could have been her meaning when she said "I think you may see me—before that."

Only once on the run to Honolulu was the flotilla of transports neared by other voyagers. Three days out from San Francisco the "O. and O." liner Doric slowly overhauled and gradually passed them by. Exchanging signals, "All well on board," she was soon lost in the shadows of the night long miles ahead.

CHAPTER VII

There was trouble at the Presidio.

All but ten of the escaped prisoners had been recaptured or self-surrendered, but the ten still at large were among the worst of the array, and among the ten was the burly, hulking recruit enlisted under the name of Murray, but declared by Captain Kress, on the strength of the report of a detective from town, to be earlier and better known as Sackett and as a former member of the Seventh Cavalry, from which regiment he had parted company without the formality of either transfer or discharge.

Murray was a man worth his keep, as military records of misdemeanors went, and a sore-hearted fellow was the sergeant of the guard, held responsible for the wholesale escape. And yet it was not so much the sergeant's fault. The evening had come on dark, damp, and dripping. Gas-lamps and barrack-lanterns were lighted before the sunset gun. The sergeant himself and several of the guard had been called inside to the prison room by the commanding officer and his staff. There was a maze of brick and wooden buildings in front of the guard-house, and a perfect tangle of dense shrubbery only fifty yards away to the west. It was into this that most of the fugitives dived and were instantly lost to sight, while others had doubled behind the guard-house and rushed into an alley-way that passed in rear of the club and a row of officers' quarters.

Some of them apparently had taken refuge in the cellars or wood-and coal-sheds until thick darkness came down, and others had actually dared to enter the quarters of Lieutenant Ray, for the back door was found wide open, the sideboard, wherein had been kept some choice old Kentucky whiskey produced only on special occasions, had been forced, and the half-emptied demijohn and some glasses stood on the table in a pool of sloppy water.

But what was worse, the lieutenant's desk in the front room, securely locked when he went to town, had been burst open with a chisel, and Mr. Ray had declined to say how much he had lost. Indeed, he did not fully know.

"Too busy to come in," was the message he had sent his mother the morning after the discovery, and yet all that morning he remained about his quarters after one brief interview with the perturbed and exasperated post commander, ransacking desks, drawers, and trunks in the vain hope that he might find in them some of the missing property, for little by little the realization was forced upon him that his loss would sum up several hundreds—all through his own neglect and through disregard of his father's earnest counsel.

Only three days before the lieutenant commanding his troop had been sent to Oregon and Washington on duty connected with the mustering of volunteers,—their captain was a field officer of one of the regiments of his native State,—and, in hurriedly leaving, Lieutenant Creswell had turned over to his young subordinate not only the troop fund, amounting to over four hundred dollars, but the money belonging to the post athletic association, and marked envelopes containing the pay of certain soldiers on temporary detached service—

Charles King

in all between nine hundred and one thousand dollars.

"Whenever you have care of public money—even temporarily—put it at once into the nearest United States depository," said his father. "Even office safes in garrison are not safe," he had further said. "Clerks, somehow, learn the combination and are tempted sometimes beyond their strength. Lose no time, therefore, in getting your funds into the bank."

And that was what he meant to do in this case, only, as the absent troopers were expected to return in two days, what was the use of breaking up those sealed envelopes and depositing the whole thing only to have to draw it out in driblets again as the men came to him for it. Surely he could safely leave that much at least in the quartermaster's safe. Creswell never thought of depositing the cash at all. He carried it around with him, a wad of greenbacks and a little sack of gold, and never lost a cent.

Ray took the entire sum to the quartermaster's office Tuesday evening and asked to store it in the safe. The clerk looked up from his desk and said he was sorry, but the quartermaster was the only man who knew the combination, and he had gone over to Camp Merritt.

So Ray kept it that night and intended taking it to town Wednesday morning, but drills interposed. He carried a little fortune with him when he went in to meet his mother and sister Wednesday evening, half intending to ask the genial "major,"—mine host of the Occidental,—to take care of it for him in the private safe, but the major was out and the money was still bulging in Ray's pockets when he returned to the post late that night, and it had been very much in his way. Thursday he fully expected the troopers back, and yet when stables were over Thursday evening and he was ready to start for town to join his dear ones, and was arraying himself in his most immaculate uniform and secretly rejoicing in the order prohibiting officers from wearing for the time being civilian dress, he found himself still burdened by the money packages and in a hurry to catch a certain car or else keep them waiting for dinner.

The quartermaster's office was several hundred yards away, and there stood his own desk, a beautiful and costly thing—his mother's gift—with its strong locks and intricate system of pigeon-holes and secret drawers. He would "chance it" one night, he said, and give his trusted servant orders to stand guard over the premises, and so the little bag of gold went into one closed compartment, the envelopes and wads of treasury notes into the hidden drawer, and the key into his watch-pocket.

His servant was a young man whose father had been with Colonel Ray for quarter of a century, a faithful Irishman by the name of Hogan. He was honest to the core and had but one serious failing—he *would* drink. He would go for months without a lapse, and then something would happen to give him a start, and nothing short of a spree would satisfy his craving. It was said that in days gone by "old man Hogan" was similarly afflicted, but those were times when an occasional frolic was the rule rather than the exception with most troopers on the far frontier, and Hogan senior had followed the fortunes of the—th Cavalry and Captain Ray until an Indian bullet had smashed his bridle-arm and compelled his discharge.

Whereupon Mrs. Ray had promptly told the gallant fellow that their army home was to be his, and that if he would consent to serve as butler or as the captain's own man to look after his boots, spurs, and sabres he would never lack for money comforts, or home.

Perhaps had Mrs. Ray foreseen that the dashing Irishman was destined to lay siege to the heart of her pretty maid, she might have suggested setting Hogan up in business farther away. Perhaps, too, she would not, for his almost pathetic devotion to her beloved husband was something she could never forget. Hogan, the crippled veteran, and Kitty, the winsome maid, were duly wed, and continued as part of the army household wherever they went. And in course of the quarter century it seemed to be but a case of domestic history repeating itself that young "Mart" should become Mr. Sandy's factotum and valet, even though Sandy could have secured the services of a much better one for less money. Young Mart had all his father's old-time dash and impetuosity, but less of his devotion, and on this particular Thursday evening, just when his master most needed him, Mart was not to be found. Ray stormed a bit as he finished his toilet. Then, as there was no time to be lost, he closed the door of his bedroom behind him and hastened away to the east gate. Just outside the reservation was a resort kept by a jovial compatriot of Hogan's,—assuming that an Irishman is always an Irishman whether born on the sod or in the States,—and there Ray felt pretty sure of finding his servant and sending him home to mount guard. And there, sure enough, he learned that Hogan had been up to within five minutes, and had left saying he must go to help the lieutenant. He was perfectly sober, said the publican, and it was more than half a mile back to quarters. Ray would be late for dinner as it was, the car was coming, and so, though dissatisfied and ill at ease, he jumped aboard, hurried to the Occidental, and within three hours was stunned and almost crushed by the tidings that the house had been entered and robbed, probably within an hour after he left it.

And now Saturday morning, while the guns of Alcatraz were booming in salute across the bay and all the garrison was out along the shore or on the seaward heights, waving farewell to the Vinton flotilla, and his mother and Maidie had gone out with the department commander to bid them god-speed, poor Sandy sat wretchedly in his quarters.

Hogan, overwhelmed by the magnitude of his master's misfortune, and realizing that it was due in no small degree to his own neglect, was now self-exiled from the lieutenant's roof, and seeking such consolation as he could find at the Harp of Erin outside the walls, a miserable and contrite man,—contrite, that is to say, as manifested in the manner of his country, for Hogan was pottle deep in his distress.

Although vouched for as perfectly sober from the Hibernian point of view, he well knew that he had taken so much that fatal Thursday evening as to be fearful of meeting his master, and so had kept out of the way until full time for him to be gone to dinner. Then, working his way homeward in the darkness of the night, he had marvelled much at finding the back door open, rejoiced at sight of the demijohn and disorder in the little dining-room, arguing therefrom that the lieutenant had had some jovial callers and therefore hadn't missed him.

Hogan drank, in his master's priceless old Blue Grass Bourbon, to the health of the party, and then, stumbling into the bedroom and lighting the lamp, came upon a sight that filled him with dismay—the beautiful desk burst open, drawers and letters and papers scattered about in utter confusion,—and in his excitement and terror he had gone on the run to the adjutant's quarters, told that official of his discovery, and then learned of the wholesale jail delivery that occurred at retreat.

He wrung his hands and wept as he listened to his young master's wrathful rebuke and the recital of his losses. He hung meekly about the house all night long, but, unable to

bear the sight of poor Ray's mingled anger and distress, he
had fled with the coming of the day and gone to tell his woes
to his friend of the Harp.

Afternoon of Saturday came, and still Ray sat there
nerveless.

He knew that any moment now would bring that loving
mother and sister. He had cleared up the litter left by the
robbers, put his desk in order, and Hogan had done his best
with the sideboard in the other room.

Sympathetic souls among his brother officers had been in
from time to time consoling him with theories that the thief
could not escape,—would surely be recaptured and the
money recovered. But on the other hand he was visited by
the returned troopers in quest of their money, and was
compelled to tell them of the robbery and to ask them to wait
until Monday, when he would be able to pay them.

Luckier than others who have been overtaken in the army by
somewhat similar misfortune, Ray knew that he had only to
acquaint his parents with the extent of his loss, and, even
though the sum was great, it would be instantly made good.
Yet the thought of having to tell his mother was a sore thing.
He had disregarded his father's caution. He had proved
unworthy of trust before the gloss had begun to wear from
his first shoulder-straps, and he well knew that his mother's
fortune was no longer what it was at the time of her
marriage.

In the years of their wanderings all over the West all her
business affairs had been in the hands of a trusted agent at
home, and it so often happens that in the prolonged absence
of owners trusted agents follow the lead of the unjust
steward of Holy Writ and make friends of the mammon of

unrighteousness and ducks and drakes of their employers' assets.

The ranch bought for him the year gone by was a heavy drain. His father, in giving him a few hundred dollars for his outfit, had told him that now he must live entirely on his pay, and that he should be able to "put by" a little every month.

But, as was to be expected of his father's son and his Kentucky blood, Sandy could not bid farewell to his associates at the ranch or the citizens of the little cow and mining town on the Big Horn without a parting "blow out," in which his health was drunk a dozen times an hour. Oh, that he had that money now instead of certain unpaid bills in that ravished secret drawer! It was humiliation inexpressible to have to send those men away empty-handed, and in his dejection and misery, poor boy, he wandered to his sideboard instead of going to luncheon at the mess, and all he had had to eat or drink that day, by the time Mrs. Ray and Maidie came late in the afternoon, was some crackers and cheese and he didn't know how many nips of that priceless Blue Grass Bourbon.

The bright, brave young eyes were glassy and his dark cheek heavily flushed when at four o'clock he hastened out to assist his mother from her carriage, and the color fled from her beautiful face; her heart seemed to stand still and her hand trembled violently as she noted it all, but took his arm without a word, and, with Maidie silently following, went up the steps and into the little army home, where the door closed behind them, and the knot of lookers-on, officers awaiting the call for afternoon stables, glanced significantly at each other, then went on their way.

CHAPTER VIII

Vinton's flotilla came steaming into Honolulu harbor just as the smoke of the Doric was fading away on the westward horizon.

Cheers and acclamations, a banquet tendered to the entire force in the beautiful grounds about the Palace, and a welcome such as even San Francisco had not given awaited them. Three days were spent in coaling for the long voyage to Manila, and during that time officers and men were enabled to spend hours in sea-bathing and sight-seeing.

Vinton, eager to push ahead, fumed with impatience over the slow and primitive methods by which his ships were coaled, but the junior officers found many a cause for rejoicing over their enforced detention. Dinners, dances, and surf-rides were the order of every evening. Riding parties to the Pali and picnics at Pearl Harbor and the plantations along the railway filled up every hour of the long, soft, sensuous days.

The soldiers explored every nook and corner of the town and, for a wonder, got back to ship without serious diminution in their number, and with a high opinion of the police, who seemed bent on protecting the blue-coats from the States and making the best of their exuberance of spirits.

Only one row of any consequence occurred within the forty-eight hours of their arrival. Three of the Colorado volunteers playing billiards in a prominent resort were deliberately annoyed and insulted by some merchant sailors who had been drinking heavily at the expense of a short, thick-set, burly fellow in a loud check suit and flaming necktie, a stranger to the police, who knew of him only that he had landed from the Doric and was waiting the coming of the Miowera from Vancouver for Australia, and she was due on the morrow.

He had taken quarters at a second-rate sailors' lodging-house and at first kept much to himself, but, once started to drinking with his maritime neighbors, he became noisy and truculent, and sallied forth with four of his new-found friends, all half drunk and wholly bent on mischief.

The sight of three quiet-mannered young fellows playing pool in the saloon was just the thing to excite all the blackguard instinct latent in their half-sodden skins, and from sneering remark they had rapidly passed to deliberate insult.

In less than a minute thereafter the three young volunteers, flushed and panting, were surveying the police and bystanders busily engaged in dragging out from under the tables and propping up some wrecks of humanity, while the head devil of the whole business, the burly civilian in the loud-checked suit, pitched headlong out of the rear window, was stanching the blood from his broken nose at the hydrant of a neighboring stable.

The volunteers were escorted to the landing with all honors, and their antagonists, barring the ringleader, to the police station. The affair was over so quickly that few had seen anything of it and only one man had pitched in to the support of the soldiers—a civilian who came over on the Vanguard by the authority of General Vinton, the ex-brakeman of the Southern Pacific. While the Colorado men had little to say beyond the statement that they had been wantonly insulted if not actually assailed by a gang of strangers, the railway man was ablaze with excitement and wrath over the escape of the leader of the vanquished party.

"I've seen that cur-dog face of his somewhere before," said he, "and the quicker you find him and nab him the better. That man's wanted in more than one place, or I'm a duffer."

And so the police spent hours that night in search of the stranger, but to no purpose. He kept in hiding somewhere, and their efforts were vain. Search of his luggage at the lodging-house revealed the fact that he had a lot of new shirts, underwear, etc., but not a paper or mark that revealed his identity. The proprietor said the man had given the name of Spence, but he heard two of the sailors call him Sackett.

The following evening the general and his staff dined at the beautiful home of one of the old and wealthy residents, and towards nine o'clock Mr. Stuyvesant asked his general's permission to withdraw, as he had two calls to make before returning aboard ship. They were to sail at dawn.

Bidding good-night and good-by to his charming hostess, and declining the hospitable offer of a post-prandial "peg" from her genial lord, the young officer stepped blithely away down the moonlit avenue.

It was a beautiful summer night. The skies were cloudless, the air soft and still. Somewhere, either at the park or in the grounds of the Royal Hawaiian, the famous band of Honolulu was giving a concert, and strains of glorious music, rich and full, came floating on the gentle breeze. Here and there the electric lights were gleaming in the dense tropical foliage, and sounds of merry chat and musical laughter fell softly on the ear.

The broad thoroughfare of Beretania Street was well nigh deserted, though once in a while the lights of a cab on noiseless wheel flashed by, and at rare intervals Stuyvesant met or overtook some blissful pair whispering in the deep shadows of the overhanging trees.

It was quite a walk to the consul-general's, his first objective point, but he enjoyed it and the brief visit that followed. Naturally the affair of the previous evening came up for discussion, and there was some conjecture and speculation as to the identity of the leader of the attack on the Denver boys. Stuyvesant repeated what his friend the brakeman said, that somewhere he had seen the fellow's face before, but he had only a second's glimpse of it, for the moment he launched in to the aid of the volunteers the man in the check suit caught sight of him—and a simultaneous crack on the nose that sent him reeling towards the open window, through which he darted the instant he could recover balance, leaving the field equally divided, four to four in point of numbers, but otherwise with overwhelming advantage on the side of the clear heads and trained muscles of the soldiers.

A grewsome sight those sailors had presented when called up for sentence in the morning, and a remorseful quartette they proved. Moreover, to the consul-general, who had been called in in the interest of fair play for Jack, they declared that they were innocent of all evil intent. They only went in for a little fun with the soldiers. It was that San Francisco fellow who called himself Spence when he was sober and Sackett when he got drunk who brought on the row, and then abandoned them to their fate. He had owned that he "had it in" for soldiers in general,—hated the whole gang of them and wanted to see them well licked. He had plenty of money and would pay their fines if the police "ran them in," and now he had left them in the lurch.

They had no money and were confronted with the probability of a month's labor with the "chain-gang" on the public roads if the consul-general couldn't get them off. So that amiable official had gone out to the flotilla and had a talk with the Colorado officers and the three brawny heroes of the billiard-room battle, with the result that everybody agreed to heap all the blame on the vanished culprit in the check suit, and the sailors got off with a nominal fine and went home to nurse their bruises and their wrath against Spence, *alias* Sackett. That fellow shouldn't get away on the Miowera if they could help it.

All this Stuyvesant was pondering over as, after stopping to leave his P. P. C. at the Pacific Club, he strolled down Fort Street on his way to the boat-landing. The big whistle of an incoming steamer had attracted his attention as he left the consul-general's to make one more call, and at the club he heard someone say the Miowera had reached her dock and would sail for Australia in the morning.

The sky, that had been so cloudless early in the evening, became somewhat overcast by eleven, and the moonlight was dim and vague as he reached the landing.

In his several trips to and from the transport it happened that he had fallen frequently into the hands of a bright Kanaka boatboy whose admirable rowing and handling of the boat had pleased and interested him.

"Be ready to take me out about 11.30," he had told him, and now where was he?

Several officers and soldiers were there bargaining with the boatmen, and three or four of these amphibious Hawaiians precipitated themselves on Stuyvesant with appeals for a job, but he asked for Joe.

"Him gone," was the answer of an eager rival. "Him other job;" but even as they would have persuaded Stuyvesant that Joe was not to be had and his selection must be one of their number, Joe himself came running from the direction of a warehouse a short pistol-shot away.

"What kept you, Joe?" asked Stuyvesant, as the light boat danced away on the tide.

"Feller want me take him outside Miowera," was the answer, "him behind warehouse."

"The deuce you say!" exclaimed Stuyvesant, turning about in the stern-sheets and gazing back to shore. "Are there landing-stairs at the warehouse, and is he waiting for you there?"

"Huh," nodded Joe.

"Then here," said Stuyvesant, glancing moon-ward and noting with satisfaction that the luminary was behind a thick bank of clouds. "Turn back and row to the warehouse steps. I want to look at that fellow." So saying, he quickly threw off his uniform coat with its gleaming shoulder-straps and collar device, stowed his forage-cap under the seat, and sat bareheaded and in his shirt-sleeves.

Obedient to Joe's powerful strokes, the little boat was speedily gliding in among the shadows of the sailing-ships moored along the quay, and presently her stern was swung round to a flight of stone steps, and Stuyvesant bounded ashore. Over at the boat-landing the electric lights were gleaming and the sound of many voices chaffering over boat-fares was heard. Here among the sheds and warehouses all was silence and darkness, but Stuyvesant unhesitatingly strode straight to the corner of the big building and into the blackness of the westward side, peering right and left in search of the skulker who dared not come to the open dock, yet sought means of reaching the Australian steamer.

For a moment he could distinguish no living object, then paused to listen, and within ten seconds was rewarded. Somewhere close at hand between him and a low shed to his left there was the sound of sudden collision and a muttered oath. Some invisible body had bumped against some invisible box, and, turning sharply, Stuyvesant made a spring, and the next instant had grappled with some burly, powerful form, and was dragging it, despite furious resistance, towards the light.

He was conscious of the sickening odor of sour whiskey, of a volley of mad threats and imprecations, of a stinging blow in the face that only served to make him cling the tighter to his prisoner. Then, as they swayed and struggled to and fro, he felt that he was not gaining ground, and that this unseen ruffian might after all escape him. He lifted up his voice in a mighty shout:

"Police! Police! This way!"

Then he heard a savage oath, a sputtering, savage "Let go, damn your soul!" and then felt a sharp, stinging pang in the right side—another—another! and earth and sky reeled as his grasp relaxed, and with a moan of anguish he sank fainting on the dock.

CHAPTER IX

Vinton's fleet had reached Manila. A third expedition had coaled at Honolulu and gone on its way. More transports were coming, and still there lingered in this lovely land of sun and flowers—lingered for a time 'twixt life and death— Vinton's stricken aide-de-camp, Lieutenant Stuyvesant.

Of his brutal antagonist no trace had been found. The shrill cries of the Kanaka boat-boy, supplementing the young officer's stentorian shout for the police, had brought two or three Hawaiian star-bearers and club-wielders to the scene of that fierce and well-nigh fatal struggle. All they found was the gallant victim writhing in pain upon the dock, his hand pressed to his side and covered with the blood that poured from his wounds.

It was half an hour before a surgeon reached them, rowed in with the general from the Vanguard. By that time conscious-ness had fled and, through loss of the vital fluid, Stuyvesant's pulse was well-nigh gone. They bore him to the Royal Hawaiian, where a cool and comfortable room could be had, and there, early on the following morning, and to the care of local physicians, the general was compelled to leave him.

With the brakeman to aid them, the police searched every nook and corner of the Miowera, and without result. Murray, *alias* Spence, *alias* Sackett, fugitive from justice, could not be aboard that ship unless he had burrowed beneath the coal in the bunkers, in which event the stokers promised he should be shovelled into the furnaces as soon as discovered. Every sailor's lodging in the town was ransacked, but to no purpose: Murray could not be found.

For a fortnight Stuyvesant's fate was in doubt. Officers of the third expedition could carry with them to Manila only the hope that he might recover. Not until the ships of the fourth flotilla were sighted was the doctor able to say that the chances were now decidedly in his favor.

He was lifted into a reclining chair the day of the flag-raising—that pathetic ceremony in which, through tear-dimmed eyes, the people saw their old and much-loved emblem supplanted by the stars and stripes of their new hope and aspirations. He was sitting up, languid, pallid, and grievously thin, when the tidings reached him that the transport with six troops of the—th Cavalry among others had arrived, and the doctor, with a quizzical grin on his genial face, informed his patient that some Red Cross nurses were with the command, and that two very nice-looking young women, in their official caps, aprons, and badges, were at that moment inquiring at the office if they could not see the invalid officer and be of some service to him.

Sore in body and spirit, wrathful at the fate that robbed him of a share of the glory he felt sure awaited his comrades at Manila, Stuyvesant was in no humor for a joke and plainly showed it. He gave it distinctly to be understood that he needed no coddling of any kind and preferred not to see the ladies, no matter what they belonged to. Not to put too fine a point upon it, Mr. Stuyvesant said he didn't "wish to be bothered," and this was practically the reply that reached two very earnest, kind-hearted young women, for the attendant, scenting the possible loss of a big fee if he should be supplanted by superior attractions, communicated the invalid's exact words to the Red Cross nurses, and they went back, wounded, to their ship.

Stuyvesant's room was on the ground-floor in one of the outlying cottages, and its Venetian blinds opened on the broad and breezy veranda. It was far more quiet and retired than apartments in the main building, the rooms overhead being vacant and the occupants of that which adjoined his having left for San Francisco within a day or two of his coming.

"I feel too forlorn to see anybody," was his explanation to the doctor. "So don't let anybody in." But several officers from the transport got leave to come ashore and take quarters at the Hawaiian. The rooms above had to be given to them, and their resounding footsteps made him wince.

"There's two ladies to take this next-door room," said his garrulous attendant that afternoon, and Stuyvesant thought opprobrious things. "They'll be giggling and talking all night, I suppose," said he disgustedly when the "medico" came in late that afternoon. "I wish you'd move me, if you can't them."

The doctor went and consulted the head of the house. "Certainly," said that affable Boniface. "If Mr. Stuyvesant is well enough to be carried up one flight I can give him a larger, airier room with bath attached, where he'll be entirely isolated. It was too expensive for our visitors from the transports, but— I believe you said Mr. Stuyvesant—wouldn't mind"—a tentative at which the doctor looked wise and sagely winked.

When that able practitioner returned to the cottage two young women with Red Cross badges were seated on the veranda, just in from a drive, apparently, and a dark-eyed little chap in the uniform of a subaltern of the cavalry was with them. They had drawn their chairs into the shade and close to the Venetian blinds, behind which in his darkened room reclined the languid patient.

"That will drive him simply rabid," said the doctor to himself, and prepared a professional smile with which to tell the glad tidings that he should be borne forthwith to higher regions.

He had left Stuyvesant peevish, fretful, but otherwise inert, asking only to be spared from intrusion. He found him alert, attent, eager, his eyes kindling, his cheeks almost flushing. The instant the doctor began to speak the patient checked him and bent his ear to the sound of soft voices and laughter from without.

"I've fixed it all," whispered the medical man reassuringly. "We'll move you in a minute—just as soon as I can call in another man or two," and he started for the door, whereat his erratic patient again uplifted a hand and beckoned, and the doctor tip-toed to his side and bent his ear and looked puzzled, perturbed, but finally pleased. Stuyvesant said that, thinking it all over, he "guessed" he would rather stay where he was.

And then, when the doctor was gone, what did he do but take a brace in his chair and bid the attendant go out and say to the officer on the veranda, Lieutenant Ray, that Mr. Stuyvesant would be very glad to speak with him if he'd be so kind as to come in, whereat the soft laughter suddenly ceased.

There was a sound of light footsteps going in one direction and a springy, soldierly step coming in the other. Then entered

Mr. Sanford Ray, with outstretched hands, and the attendant, following and peering over his shoulder, marvelled at the sudden change that had come over his master.

Three days later, when the City of Sacramento was pronounced ready to proceed, and the officers and Red Cross nurses *en route* to Manila were warned to rejoin the ship, Lieutenant Stuyvesant "shook," so to speak, his civil physician, persuaded the army surgeons with the fleet that a sea-voyage was all he needed to make a new man of him, and was carried aboard the Sacramento and given an airy stateroom on the upper deck, vacated in his favor by one of the ship's officers,—consideration not made public, but Claus Spreckles & Co., bankers, had never before received such a deposit from this very able seaman in all the years he had been sailing or steaming in and out of Honolulu harbor.

And now retribution overtook the invalid. The Red Cross had made a marvellous name for itself in San Francisco, and was already organized and doing wonders at Honolulu. Its ministrations had been gladly accepted by the scores of officers and men among the volunteers, to whom the somewhat bare and crude conditions of camp hospitals were doubtless very trying. Women of gentlest birth and most refined associations donned its badge and dress and wrought in ward, kitchen, or refectory. It was a noble and patriotic purpose that inspired such sacrifice.

It was a joy to the embryo soldiery to be fed and comforted day by day with the delicacies of the Red Cross tables; but there were military magnates and martinets who dared to question the wisdom of such preparation for the stern scenes of campaigning ahead of the volunteers, and who presumed to point out to the officers of this great and far-reaching charity that, while they were most grateful for such dainties for the invalids of their command, the daily spectacle of scores of lusty, hearty young heroes feasting at the tables of the Red Cross, to the neglect of their own simple but sufficient rations, prompted the query as to what the boys would do without the Red Cross when they got into the field and couldn't have cake and pie and cream with their coffee.

The Red Cross, very properly, took umbrage at such suggestions and branded the suggesters as horrid. The Red Cross had done such widespread good and was ready to do so much more that criticism of its methods was well-nigh unbearable. And now that it had obtained the sanction of the government to send out to Manila not only supplies and dainties of every possible kind, but dozens of its members to serve as nurses to the sick and wounded, it scored a triumph over rival organizations, notably the Patriotic Daughters of America, whose vice-president, the austere Miss Perkins, first bombarded the papers in vain protest and denunciation, the Red Cross being her main objective, and with abuse of the commanding officers in camp; then called in person on the same officers to demand transportation to Manila with the next expedition.

The Red Cross held its head very high, and with reason. It ruffled its feathers and resented any slight. It sometimes mistook courteous protest against its lavish gifts to such soldiers as were in no wise needy as vicious and unhallowed criticism, and occasionally—*only* occasionally—it grievously enlarged and exaggerated alleged slights received at the hands of luckless officials. And then even those soft and shapely hands could develop cat-like claws, and the soothing voices take on an acid and scathing intonation, and the eyes, so ready to moisten with pity and sympathy at the sight of suffering, could shoot spiteful little fires at the objects of such divine displeasure, and poor Stuyvesant's petulant words, wrung from him in a moment of exasperation and never intended to reach the fair band of sisters of the Cross, were piled high with additions, impolitic, impolite, discourteous, impudent, intolerable, yes, even profane and blasphemous.

Eleven of the twelve Red Cross nurses, packed three in a room aboard the Sacramento, swore they would not have anything to do with Mr. Stuyvesant. The twelfth, the one soldier's daughter in the band, said nothing at all.

"Well, now, Miss Ray, *don't* you think it was most discourteous, most ungentlemanly, in him to send such a message?" demanded a flushed and indignant young woman, one of the most energetic of the sisterhood, as they stood together on the promenade deck in the shade of the canvas awnings, shunning the glare of the August sun.

"Are you sure such a message was sent?" was the serious reply.

"Sure? Why, *certainly* he did! and by his own servant, too!" was the wrathful answer. "Didn't he, Miss Porter?"

And Miss Porter, the damsel appealed to, and one of the two nurses who sent in their message from the office, promptly assented. Miss Ray looked unconvinced.

"Servants, you know, sometimes deliver messages that were never sent," she answered with quiet decision. "We have seen quite a little of that in the army, and it is my father's rule to get all the facts before passing judgment. My brother thought Mr. Stuyvesant's attendant garrulous and meddlesome."

"But I asked him if he was sure that was what Mr. Stuyvesant said," persisted Miss Porter, bridling, "and he answered they were just the very words."

"And still I doubt his having sent them as a message," said Miss Ray, with slight access of color, and that evening she walked the deck long with a happy subaltern and added to her unpopularity.

There were several well-informed and pleasant women, maids and matrons both, in the little sisterhood, but somehow "the boys" did not show such avidity to walk or chat with them as they did with Miss Ray. She sorely wanted a talk with Sandy that evening, but the Belgic had come in from 'Frisco only six hours before they sailed and huge bags of letters and papers were transferred from her to the Sacramento.

There were letters for Maidie and Sandy both,—several,— but there was one bulky missive for him that she knew to be from her father, from far-away Tampa, and the boy had come down late to dinner. They had seats at the table of the commanding officer, a thing Maidie had really tried to avoid, as she felt that it discriminated, somehow, against the other nurses, who, except Mrs. Doctor Wells, their official head, were distributed about the other tables, but the major had long known and loved her father, and would have it so. This night, their first out from Honolulu, he had ordered wine-glasses on the long table and champagne served, and when dinner was well-nigh over, noticed for the first time that Ray had turned his glass down.

"Why, Sandy," he cried impulsively, "it is just twenty-two years ago this summer that your father made the ride of his life through the Indian lines to save Wayne's command on the Cheyenne. Now, there are just twenty-two of us here at table, and I wanted to propose his health and promotion. Won't you join us?"

The boy colored to the roots of his dark hair. His eyes half filled. He choked and stammered a moment and then—back went the head with the old familiar toss that was so like his father, and through his set lips Sandy bravely spoke:

"Can't, major. I swore off—to-day!"

"All right, my boy, that ends it!" answered the major heartily, while Marion, her eyes brimming, barely touched her lips to the glass, and longed to be on Sandy's side of the table that she might steal a hand to him in love and sympathy and sisterly pride. But he avoided even her when dinner was over, and was busy, he sent word, with troop papers down between-decks, and she felt, somehow, that that letter was at the bottom of his sudden resolution and longed to see it, yet could not ask.

At three bells, half-past nine, she saw him coming quickly along the promenade-deck, and she stopped her escort and held out a detaining hand.

"You'll come and have a little talk with me, won't you, Sandy?" she pleaded. "I'll wait for you as long as you like."

"After I've seen Stuyvesant awhile," he answered hurriedly. "He isn't so well. I reckon he must have overdone it," and away he went with his springy step until he reached the forward end of the promenade, where he tapped at the stateroom door. The surgeon opened it and admitted him.

His eyes were grave and anxious when, ten minutes later, he reappeared. "Norris is with him," he said in low tone, as he looked down into the sweet, serious, upturned face. "He shouldn't have tried it. He fooled the doctors completely. I'll tell you more presently," he added, noting that Mrs. Wells, with two or three of the band, were bearing down upon him for tidings of the invalid, and Sandy had heard,—as who had not?—the unfavorable opinions entertained by the sisterhood of his luckless, new-found friend.

"The doctor says he mustn't be both—I mean disturbed—wants to get him to sleep, you know," was his hurried and not too happy response to the queries of the three. "Matter of business he wanted to ask me about, that's all," he called back, as he broke away and dodged other inquiries. Once in the little box of a stateroom to which he and a fellow subaltern had been assigned, he bolted the door, turned on the electric light, and took from under his pillow a packet of letters and sat him down to read. There was one from his mother, written on her way back to Leavenworth, which he pored over intently and then reverently kissed. Later, and for the second time, he unfolded and read the longest letter his father had ever penned. It was as follows:

"I have slipped away from camp and its countless interruptions and taken a room at the hotel to-night, dear Sandy, for I want to have a long talk with my boy,—a talk we ought to have had before, and it is my fault that we didn't. I shrank from it somehow, and now am sorry for it.

"Your frank and manful letter, telling me of your severe loss and of the weakness that followed, reached me two days ago. Your mother's came yesterday, fonder than ever and pleading for you as only mothers can. It is a matter that has cost us all dear financially, but, thanks to that loving mother, you were promptly enabled to cover the loss and save your name. You know and realize the sacrifices she had to make, and she tells me that you insisted on knowing. I am glad you did, my boy. I am going to leave in your hands the whole matter of repayment.

"A young fellow of twenty can start in the army with many a worse handicap than a debt of honor and a determination to work it off. That steadies him. That matter really gives me less care than you thought for. It is the other—your giving way to an impulse to drink—that fills me with concern. You come up like a man, admit your fault, and say you deserve and expect my severe censure. Well, I've thought it all over, Sandy. My heart and my arms go out to you in your distress and humiliation, and—I have not one word of reproach or blame to give you.

"For now I shall tell you what I had thought to say when your graduation drew nigh, had we been able to master mechanics and molecules and other mathematical rot as useful to a cavalry officer as a binocular to a blind man, and that I ought to have told you when you started out for yourself as a young *ranchero*, but could not bring myself to it so long as you seemed to have no inclination that way. Times, men, and customs have greatly changed in the last forty or fifty years, my boy, and greatly for the better. Looking back over my boyhood, I can recall no day when wine was not served on your grandfather's table. The brightest minds and bravest men in all Kentucky pledged each other day and night in the cup that sometimes cheers and ofttimes inebriates, and no public occasion was complete without champagne and whiskey in abundance, no personal or private transaction considered auspicious unless appropriately 'wet.'"

"Those were days when our statesmen revelled in sentiment and song, and drank and gambled with the fervor of the followers of the races. I was a boy of tender years then, and often, with my playmates, I was called from our merry games to join the gentlemen over their wine and drain a bumper to our glorious 'Harry of the West,' and before I went to the Point, Sandy, I knew the best, and possibly the worst, whiskeys made in

Kentucky,—we *all* did,—and the man or youth who could not stand his glass of liquor was looked upon as a milksop or pitied, and yet, after all, respected, as a 'singed cat,'—a fellow who owned that John Barleycorn was too much for him, and he did not dare a single round with him.

"Then came the great war, and wars are always in one way demoralizing. West Point in the early sixties was utterly unlike the West Point of to-day, and no worse than a dozen of our greatest colleges. The corps still had its tales and traditions of the old time Fourth-of-July dinners at the mess hall, when everybody made a dash for the decanters and drank everything in sight. It was the only day in the year on which wine was served. It was in my time the invariable custom for the superintendent to receive the Board of Visitors on the day of their arrival at his quarters and to invite the officers and the graduating class to meet them, and to set forth, as for years had been the fashion at Washington, wine and punch in abundance, and the very officers detailed as our instructors would laughingly invite and challenge the youngsters so soon to shed the gray and wear the blue to drink with them again and again. I have seen dozens of the best and bravest of our fellows come reeling and shouting back to barracks, and a thoughtless set of boys laughing and applauding.

"I was stationed at the Point soon after graduation, and the men who drank were the rule, not the exception. Social visits were rarely exchanged without the introduction of the decanter. The marvel is that so many were 'temperate in our meat and drink,' as my father and grandfather used to plead when, regularly every morning, the family and the negro servants were mustered for prayers. At every post where I was stationed, either in the East or where I was most at home,—the far frontier,—whiskey was the established custom, and man after man, fellows who had made fine records during the war, and bright boys with whom I had worn the gray at the Point, fell by the wayside and were court-martialled out of service.

"In '70 and '71 we had a Board that swept the army like a seine and relegated scores of tipplers to civil life, but that didn't stop it. Little by little the sense and manhood of our people began to tell. Little by little the feeling against stimulant began to develop at the Point. It was no longer a joke to set a fledgling officer to taste the tempter—it was a crime. Four years after I was commissioned we had only one total abstainer out of some fifty officers at the mess, and he was a man whose life and honor depended on it. Three years ago, when I went to see you, there were dozens at the mess who never drank at all, and only eight who even smoked. Athletics and rifle-practice had much to do with this, I know, but there has gradually developed all over our land, notably in those communities where the custom used to be most honored in the observance, a total revulsion of sentiment.

"Quarter of a century ago, even among many gently nurtured women, the sight of a man overcome by liquor excited only sorrow and sympathy; now it commands nothing less than abhorrence. I and my surviving contemporaries started in life under the old system. You, my dear boy, are more fortunate in having begun with the new. Among the old soldiers there are still some few votaries of Bacchus who have to count their cups most carefully or risk their commissions. Among those under forty our army has far more total abstainers than all the others in the world, and such soldiers as Grant, Crook, Merritt, and Upton, of our service, and Kitchener of Khartoum, are on record as saying that the staying powers of the teetotaller exceed those even of the temperate man, and staying power is a thing to cultivate.

"As you know, I have never banished wine from our table, my boy. Both your mother and I had been accustomed to seeing it in daily use from childhood, yet she rarely touches it, even at our dinners. But, Sanford, I sent John Barleycorn to the right about the day your blessed mother promised to be my wife, and though I always keep it in the sideboard for old comrades whose heads and stomachs are still sound, and who find it agrees with them better than wine, I never offer it to the youngsters. They don't need it, Sandy, and no more do you.

"But you come of a race that lived as did their fellow-men,—to whom cards, the bottle, and betting were everyday affairs. It would be remarkable if you never developed a tendency towards one or all of them, and it was my duty to warn you before. I mourn every hour I wasted over cards and every dollar I ever won from a comrade more than—much more than—the many hundred dollars I lost in my several years' apprenticeship to poker. It's just about the poorest investment of time a soldier can devise.

"Knowing all I do, and looking back over the path of my life, strewn as it is with the wrecks of fellow-men ruined by whiskey, I declare if I could live it over again it would be with the determination never to touch a card for money or a glass for liquor.

"And now, my own boy, let me bear the blame of this— your first transgression. You are more to us than we have ever told you. You are now your sister's guardian and knight, for, though she goes under the wing of Mrs. Dr. Wells, and, owing to her intense desire to take a woman's part we could not deny her, both your mother and I are filled with anxiety as to the result. To you we look to be her shield in every possible way. We have never ceased to thank God for the pride and joy He has given us in our children. (You yourself would delight in seeing what a tip-top little soldier Will is making.) You have ever been manful, truthful, and, I say it with pride and thankfulness unutterable, *square* as boy could be. You have our whole faith and trust and love unspeakable. You have the best and fondest mother in the world, my son. And now I have not one more word to urge or advise. Think and decide for yourself. Your manhood, under God, will do the rest.

"In love and confidence,

"Father."

When Marion came tapping timidly at the stateroom door there was for a moment no answer. Sandy's face was buried in his hands as he knelt beside the little white berth. He presently arose, dashed some water over his eyes and brows, then shot back the bolt and took his sister in his arms.

CHAPTER X

Not until the tenth day out from Honolulu was Mr. Stuyvesant so far recovered as to warrant the surgeons in permitting his being lifted from the hot and narrow berth to a steamer-chair on the starboard side. Even then it was with the caution to everybody that he must not be disturbed. The heat below and in many of the staterooms was overpowering, and officers and soldiers in numbers slept upon the deck, and not a few of the Red Cross nurses spent night after night in the bamboo and wicker reclining-chairs under the canvas awnings.

Except for the tropic temperature, the weather had been fine and the voyage smooth and uneventful. The Sacramento rolled easily, lazily along. The men had morning shower-baths and, a few at a time, salt-water plunges in big canvas tanks set fore and aft on the main deck. On the port or southern side of the promenade deck the officers sported their pajamas both day and night, and were expected to appear in khaki or serge, and consequent discomfort, only at table, on drill or duty, and when visiting the starboard side, which, abaft the captain's room, was by common consent given up to the women.

They were all on hand the morning that the invalid officer was carefully aided from his stateroom to a broad reclining-chair, which was then borne to a shaded nook beneath the stairway leading to the bridge and there securely lashed. The doctor and Mr. Ray remained some minutes with him, and the steward came with a cooling drink. Mrs. Wells, doctor by courtesy and diploma, arose and asked the surgeon if there were really nothing the ladies could do—"Mr. Stuyvesant looks so very pale and weak,"—and the sisterhood strained their ears for the reply, which, as the surgeon regarded the lady's remark as reflecting upon the results of his treatment, might well be expected to be somewhat tart.

"Nothing to-day, Mrs.—er—Dr. Wells," said the army man, half vexed, also, at being detained on way to hospital. "The fever has gone and he will soon recuperate now, provided he can rest and sleep. It is much cooler on deck and—if it's only quiet—"

"Oh, he sha'n't be bothered, if that's what you mean," interposed Dr. Wells with proper spirit. "I'm sure nobody desires to intrude in the least. I asked for my associates from a sense of duty. Most of them are capable of fanning or even reading aloud to a patient without danger of over-exciting him."

"Unquestionably, madam," responded the surgeon affably, "and when such ministrations are needed I'll let you know. Good-morning." And, lifting his stiff helmet, the doctor darted down the companion-way.

"Brute!" said the lady doctor. "No wonder that poor boy doesn't get well. Miss Ray, I marvel that your brother can stand him."

Miss Ray glanced quietly up from her book and smiled. "We have known Dr. Sturgis many years," she said. "He is brusque, yet very much thought of in the army."

But at this stage of the colloquy there came interruption most merciful—for the surgeon. The deep whistle of the steamer sounded three quick blasts. There was instant rush and scurry on the lower deck. The cavalry trumpets fore and aft rang out the assembly.

It was the signal for boat-drill, and while the men of certain companies sprang to ranks and stood in silence at attention awaiting orders, other detachments rushed to their stations at the life-rafts, and others still swarmed up the stairways or clambered over the rails, and in less than a minute every man was at his post. Quickly the staff officers made the rounds, received the reports of the detachment commanders and the boat crews, and returning, with soldierly salute, gave the results to the commanding officer, who had taken position with the captain on the bridge.

For five or ten minutes the upper deck was dotted by squads of blue-shirted soldiers, grouped in disciplined silence about the boats. Then the recall was sounded, and slowly and quietly the commands dispersed and went below.

It so happened that in returning to the forecastle about a dozen troopers passed close to where Stuyvesant lay, a languid spectator, and at sight of his pale, thin face two of them stopped, raised their hands in salute, looked first eager and pleased, and then embarrassed. Their faces were familiar, and suddenly Stuyvesant remembered. Beckoning them to come nearer, he feebly spoke:

"You were in the car-fire. I thought I knew your faces."

"Yes, sir," was the instant reply of the first. "We're sorry to see the lieutenant so badly hurt—and by that blackguard Murray too, they say. If the boys ever get hold of him, sir, he'll never have time for his prayers."

"No, nor another chance to bite," grinned the second, whom Stuyvesant now recognized as the lance corporal of artillery. "He's left his mark on both of us, sir," and, so saying, the soldier held out his hand.

In the soft and fleshy part of the palm at the base of the thumb were the scars of several wounds. It did not need an expert eye to tell that they were human-tooth marks. There were the even traces of the middle incisors, the deep gash made by the fang-like dog tooth, and between the mark of the right upper canine and those of three incisors a smooth, unscarred space. There, then, must have been a vacancy in the upper jaw, a tooth broken off or gone entirely, and Stuyvesant remembered that as Murray spoke the eye-tooth was the more prominent because of the ugly gap beside it.

"He had changed the cut of his jib considerably," faintly whispered Stuyvesant, after he had extended a kind but nerveless hand to each, "but that mark would betray him anywhere under any disguise. Was Foster ever found?"

"No, sir. They sent me back to Sacramento, but nobody could remember having seen anybody like him. I'm afraid he was drowned there at Carquinez. My battery went over with the third expedition while I was up there. That's how I happen to be with the cavalry on this trip." Then up went both hands to the caps again and both soldiers sprang to attention.

Stuyvesant, looking languidly around, saw that Mr. Ray had returned, saw, moreover, that his sister was leaning on his arm, her eyes fixed on the speaker's weather-beaten face. Again it all flashed upon him—the story of Foster's infatuation for this lovely girl, his enlistment, and then his strange and unaccountable disappearance.

"I'm sorry, men," interposed Mr. Ray in pleasant tone, "but the surgeon has ordered us not to talk with Lieutenant Stuyvesant, and I shall have to repeat his order to you. You were in the car that was burned, I suppose?"

"Yes, sir. Beg pardon—we didn't know about the doctor's orders. We're mighty glad to see the lieutenant again. Come 'long, Mellen."

"Wait," whispered Stuyvesant. "Come and see me again. I want to talk with you, and—thank you for stopping to-day."

The soldiers departed happy, and Stuyvesant turned wistfully to greet Miss Ray. She was already beyond reach of his voice, leaning on Sandy's arm and gazing steadfastly into his face. He saw Mrs. Dr. Wells coming swiftly towards him with inquiry in her eyes, and impulsively, peevishly, and in disappointment he turned again his face to the wall, as it were. At least that was not the Red Cross nurse he longed for, good and sympathetic and wise in her way as she undoubtedly was.

He wished now with all his heart that they had placed his chair so that he could look back along the promenade deck instead of forward over the forecastle at the sparkling sea. He felt that, pacing up and down together, the brother and sister must come within ten feet of his chair before they turned back, and he longed to look at her, yet could not. Sturgis had said he would return in a few minutes, and he hadn't come. Stuyvesant felt aggrieved. It would be high noon before many minutes. Already the ship officers were on the bridge ready to "take the sun," and mess-call for the men was sounding on the lower decks. He would give a fortune, thought he, to feel once more that cool, soft, slender little hand on his forehead. There were other hands, some that were certainly whiter than Miss Ray's, and probably quite as soft and cool, hands that before the report of his slur upon the Red Cross would gladly have ministered to him, but he shrank from thought of any touch but one. He would have given another fortune, if he had it, could Marion Ray but come and sit by him and talk in her cordial, pleasant tones. There were better talkers, wittier, brighter women within hail—women who kept their hearers laughing much of the time, which Miss Ray did not, yet he shrank from the possibility of one of their number accosting him.

Twice he was conscious that Dr. Wells and Miss Porter had tip-toed close and were peering interestedly at him, but he shut his eyes and would not see or hear. He did not "want to be bothered," it was only too evident, and as the ship's bell chimed the hour of noon and the watch changed, his would-be visitors slipped silently away and he was alone.

When the doctor came cautiously towards him a few minutes later, Stuyvesant was to all appearances sleeping, and the "medico" rejoiced in the success of his scheme. When, not five minutes after the doctor peeped at him, the voice of the captain was heard booming from the bridge just over the patient's pillowed head, it developed that the patient was wide awake. Perhaps what the captain said would account for this.

A dozen times on the voyage that mariner had singled out Miss Ray for some piece of attention. Now, despite the fact that almost the entire Red Cross party were seated or strolling or reclining there under the canvas awning and he must have known it, although they were hidden from his view, he again made that young lady the object of his homage. She was at the moment leaning over the rail, with Sandy by her side, gazing at the dark blue, beautiful waters that, flashing and foam-crested, went sweeping beneath her. The monarch of the ship, standing at the outer end of the bridge, had caught sight of her and gave tongue at once. A good seaman was the captain and a stalwart man, but he knew nothing of tact or discretion.

"Oh, Miss Ray," he bawled, "come up on the bridge and I'll show you the chart. Bring the lieutenant."

For an instant she hesitated, reluctant. Not even the staff of the commanding officer had set foot on that sacred perch since the voyage began, only when especially bidden or at boat or fire drill did that magnate himself presume to ascend those stairs. As for her sister nurses, though they had explored the lower regions and were well acquainted with the interior arrangement of the Sacramento, and were consumed with curiosity and desire to see what was aloft on the hurricane-deck, the stern prohibition still staring at them in bold, brazen letters, "Passengers are Forbidden upon the Bridge," had served to restrain the impulse to climb.

And now here was Captain Butt singling out Miss Ray again and ignoring the rest of them. If she could have found any reasonable excuse for refusing Maidie Ray would have declined. But Sandy's eyes said "Come." Butt renewed his invitation. She turned and looked appealingly at Mrs. Wells, as though to say "What shall I do?" but that matron was apparently engrossed in a volume of Stevenson, and would not be drawn into the matter, and finally Marion caught Miss Porter's eye. There, at least, was a gleam of encouragement and sympathy. Impulsive and capricious as that young woman could be on occasions, the girl had learned to appreciate the genuine qualities of her room-mate, and of late had been taking sides for Marion against the jealousies of her fellows.

"Why don't you go?" she murmured, with a nod of her head towards the stairs, and with slightly heightened color, Miss

Ray smiled acceptance at the captain, and, following Sandy's lead through the labyrinth of steamer-chairs about them, tripped briskly away over the open deck, and there, at the very foot of the steep, ladder-like ascent, became aware of Mr. Stuyvesant leaning on an elbow and gazing at her with all his big blue eyes.

She had to stop and go around under the stairs and take his thin, outstretched hand. She had to stop a moment to speak to him, though what he said, or she said, neither knew a moment after. All she was conscious of as she turned away was that now at least every eye in all the sisterhood was on her, and, redder than ever, she fairly flew up the steep steps, and was welcomed by the chivalric Butt upon the bridge.

That afternoon several of the Band were what Miss Porter was constrained to call "nastily snippy" in their manner to her, and, feeling wronged and misjudged, it was not to be wondered at that her father's daughter should resent it. And yet so far from exulting in having thus been distinguished and recognized above her fellows, Miss Ray had felt deeply embarrassed, and almost the first words she said after receiving the bluff seaman's effusive greeting were in plea for her associates.

"Oh, Captain Butt, it's most kind of you to ask me up here—and my brother, too, will be so interested in the chart-room, but, can't you—won't you ask Dr. Wells and at least some of the ladies? You know they all would be glad to come, and—"

"That's all right, Miss Ray," bawled old Butt, breaking in on her hurried words. "I'll ask 'em up here some other time. You see we're rolling a bit to-day, and like as not some of 'em would pitch over things, and—and—well, there ain't room for more'n three at a time anyhow."

"Then you ought to have asked Dr. Wells first and some of the seniors."—She hesitated about saying elders.—No one of the Band would have welcomed an invitation tendered on account of her advanced years.

"It'll be just as bad if I go and ask her now," said Butt testily. "The others will take offence, and life's too short for a shipmaster to be explaining to a lot of women why they can't all come at once on the bridge. I'll have 'em up to-morrow—any three you say."

But when the morrow came he didn't "have 'em up." Maidie had pleaded loyally for her associates, but was too proud or sensitive to so inform them. The captain had said he would do that, and meanwhile she tried not to feel exasperated at the injured airs assumed by several of the Band and the cutting remarks of one or two of their number.

That afternoon, however, the skies became overcast and the wind rose. That night the sea dashed high towards the rail and the Sacramento wallowed deep in the surges. Next morning the wind had freshened to a gale. All air-ports were closed. The spray swept the promenade deck along the starboard side and the Red Cross and two-thirds of the martial passenger-list forgot all minor ills and annoyances in the miseries of *mal de mer*. Three days and nights were most of the women folk cooped in their cabins, but Miss Ray was an old sailor and had twice seen far heavier weather on the Atlantic. Sheltered from the rain by the bridge-deck and from the spray and gale by heavy canvas lashed athwartship in front of the captain's room, and securely strapped in her reclining-chair, this young lady fairly rejoiced in the magnificent battle with the elements and gloried in the bursting seas. Sandy, too, albeit a trifle upset, was able to be on deck, and one of the "subs" from the port-side hearing of it, donned his outer garments and cavalry boots and joined forces with them, and Stuyvesant, hearing their merry voices, declared that he could not breathe in his stuffy cabin and demanded to be dressed and borne out on deck too. At first the surgeon said no, whereupon his patient began to get worse.

So on the second day the doctor yielded, and all that day and the third of the storm, by which time the starboard deck was slowly becoming peopled with a few spectral and barely animate feminine shapes, Stuyvesant reclined within arm's length of the dark-eyed girl who had so entranced him, studying her beauty, drinking in her words, and gaining such health and strength in the life-giving air and such bliss from the association that Sturgis contemplated with new complacency the happy result of his treatment, for when the gale subsided, and on the fourth day they ran once more into smooth and lazy waters, it was Stuyvesant's consuming desire to take up his bed and walk, except when Miss Ray was there to talk or read to him.

And this was the state of affairs when the Sacramento hove in sight of the bold headlands, green and beautiful, that front the sea at the northeast corner of mountainous Luzon. Once within soundings and close to a treacherous shore, with only Spanish authority to rely on as to rocks, reefs, and shoals, no wonder old Butt could have no women on the bridge, this, too, at the very time they most wished to be there, since everything worth seeing lay on the port or southern side, and that given up to those horrid officers and their pajamas.

Not until his anchor dropped in Manila Bay did the master of the Sacramento think to redeem his promise to bid the ladies of the Red Cross to the sacred bridge, and incidentally to tell them how Miss Ray had urged it in their behalf while they were out on blue waters, but now it was too late.

CHAPTER XI

It was late in the afternoon when the Sacramento, slowly feeling her way southward, had come within view of El Fraile and Corregidor, looming up like sentinels at the entrance to the great, far-spreading bay.

Butt and his assistants, with the field officer in command of the troops, peered through their binoculars or telescopes for sign of cruiser or transport along the rocky shores, and marvelled much that none could be seen. Over against the evening sun just sinking to the west the dim outlines of the upper masts and spars of some big vessel became visible for three minutes, then faded from view. The passengers swarmed on deck, silent, anxious, ever and anon gazing upward at the bridge as though in hope of a look or word of encouragement.

It was midsummer and more when they left Honolulu, and by this time the American force, land and naval, in front of Manila ought to be ample to overcome the Spaniards. But there was ever that vexing problem as to what Aguinaldo and his followers might do rather than see the great city given over to the Americans for law and order instead of to themselves for loot and rapine. The fact that all coast lights thus far were extinguished was enough to convince the Sacramento's voyagers that they were still unwelcome to the natives, but both the shipmaster and the cavalry officer commanding had counted on finding cruiser, or despatch boat at least, on lookout for them and ready to conduct them to safe anchorage. But no such ship appeared, and the alternative of going about and steaming out to sea for the night or dropping anchor where he lay was just presenting itself to Butt when from the lips of the second officer, who had clambered up the shrouds, there came the joyous shout: "By Jove! There's Corregidor light!"

Surely enough, even before the brief tropic twilight was over and darkness had settled down, away to the southward, at regular ten-second intervals, from the crest of the rock-bound, crumbling parapet on Corregidor Island, a brilliant light split the cloudy vista and flashed a welcome to the lone wanderer on the face of the waters. It could mean only one thing: Manila Bay was dominated by Dewey's guns. The Yankee was master of Corregidor, and had possessed himself of both fort and light-house. In all probability Manila itself had fallen.

"Half speed ahead!" was the order, and again the throb of the engines went pulsing through the ship, and the Sacramento slowly forged ahead over a smooth summer sea. At midnight the pilot and glad tidings were aboard, and at dawn the decks were thronged with eager voyagers, and a great, full-throated cheer went up from the forecastle head as the gray, ghost-like shapes of the war-ships loomed up out of the mist and dotted the unruffled surface.

But that cheer sank to nothingness beside one which followed fifteen minutes later, when the red disk of the sun came peeping over the low, fog-draped range far to the eastward and, saluted by the boom of the morning gun from the battlements of the old city, there sailed to the peak of the lofty flag-staff the brilliant colors and graceful folds of the stars and stripes.

The three-century rule of Castile and Aragon was ended. The yellow and red of Spain was supplanted by the scarlet, white, and blue of America, and in a new glory of its own "Old Glory" unfolded to the faintly rising breeze, and all along the curving shore and over the placid waters rang out the joyous, life-giving, heart-stirring notes of the Yankee reveille.

For long hours later there came launches, bancas, and cascoes from fleet and shore. The debarkation of the cavalry began in the afternoon. They had left their horses at the Presidio, six thousand miles away, and were troopers only in name. The officers who came as passengers got ashore in the course of the day and made their way to the Ayuntamiento to report their arrival and receive their assignments.

The Red Cross nurses looked in vain for the hospital launch that, it was supposed, would hasten to convey them to comfortable quarters adjoining the sick-wards or convalescent camps. They listened with the deepest interest to the description of the assault of the 13th of August that made Merritt master of Manila, and the elders, masculine and feminine, who knew something of what battle meant when American was pitted against American, looked at each other in wonderment as they heard how much had been won at cost of so little.

Sandy Ray, kissing Marion good-by and promising to see Stuyvesant in the near future, went over the side with his troop and, landing at the stone dock at the foot of the Paseo de Santa Lucia, found himself trudging along at the head of his men under massive walls nearly three centuries old, bristling with antiquated, highly ornamented Spanish guns, and streaked with slime and vegetation, while along the high parapets across the moat thousands of Spanish soldiers squatted and stared at them in sullen apathy.

Maidie's knight and champion indeed! His duty called him with his fellows to a far-away suburb up the Pasig River. Her duty held her to await the movements of the sisterhood, and what she might lack for sympathy among them was made up in manifest yet embarrassing interest on part of the tall young aide-de-camp, for Stuyvesant was bidden to remain aboard ship until suitable accommodation could be found for him ashore.

Under any other circumstances he would have objected vehemently, but, finding that the Red Cross contingent was to share his fate, and that Miss Ray was one of the dozen condemned to remain, he bore his enforced lot with Christian and soldierly resignation.

"Only," said Dr. Wells, "one would suppose that the Red Cross was entitled to some consideration, and that all preparation would have been made for our coming." It was neither flattering nor reassuring, nor, indeed, was it kind, that they should be so slighted, said the sisterhood that evening; but worse still was in store, for on the morrow, early, the Esmeralda came steaming in from Hong Kong, where, despite her roundabout voyage, the Belgic had arrived before the slow-moving Sacramento had rounded the northern point of Luzon, and, on the deck of the Esmeralda as she steered close alongside the transport, and thence on the unimpeded way to her moorings up the Pasig, in plain view of the sisterhood, tall, gaunt, austere, but triumphant, towered the form of the vice-president of the Patriotic Daughters of America.

For two days more the Sacramento remained at anchor in the bay over a mile from the mouth of the river, and for two days and nights the Red Cross remained aboard, unsought, unsummoned from the shore. The situation became more strained than ever, the only betterment arising from the fact that now there was more space and the nurses were no longer crowded three in a room. Mrs. Dr. Wells moved into that recently vacated by the cavalry commander, and Miss Ray and her now earnest friend, Miss Porter, were relieved by the desertion of their eldest sister, who pre-empted a major's stateroom on the upper deck.

Butt stirred up a new trouble by promptly coming to Miss Ray and bidding her move out of that stuffy hole below and take Major Horton's quarters, and bring Miss Porter with her "if that was agreeable."

It would have been, very, but "Miss Ray's head was level," as the purser put it, and despite the snippy and exasperating conduct of most of the sisterhood, that wise young woman pointed out to the shipmaster that theirs was a semi-military organization, and that the senior, Mrs. Dr. Wells, and one or two veteran nurses should have choice of quarters.

By this time Miss Porter's vehement championship of her charming and much misjudged friend had excited no little rancor against herself. The more she proved that they had done Miss Ray injustice, the less they liked Miss Ray's advocate. It is odd but true that many a woman finds it far easier to forgive another for being as wicked as she has declared her to be than for proving herself entirely innocent.

One thing, anyhow, Miss Porter couldn't deny, said the sisterhood,—she was accepting devoted attentions from Mr. Stuyvesant, and in her capacity as a Red Cross nurse that was inexcusable.

"Fudge!" said Miss Porter. "If it were you instead of Miss Ray he was in love with, how long would you let your badge keep him at a distance?"

The sun went down on their unappeased wrath that second night in Manila Bay, and with the morrow came added cause for disapprobation. Before the noon hour a snow-white launch with colors flying fore and aft steamed alongside, and up the stairs, resplendent, came Stuyvesant's general with a brace of staff officers, all three precipitating themselves on the invalid and, after brief converse with him, all three sending their cards to Miss Ray, who had taken refuge on the other deck.

And even while she sat reflecting what would be the wiser course, the general himself followed the card-bearer, and that distinguished warrior, with all the honors of his victorious entry fresh upon him, inclined his handsome head and begged that he might present himself to the daughter of an old and cherished friend of cadet days, and seated himself by her side with hardly a glance at the array of surrounding femininity and launched into reminiscence of "Billy Ray" as he was always called, ana it was some little time before she could say,—

"Will you let me present you to Dr. Wells, who is practically my commanding officer?" a request the general was too much of a gentleman not to accede to at once, yet looked *not* too much pleased when he was led before that commanding dame, and then distinctly displeased as, taking advantage of her opportunity, the indignant lady burst forth with her grievance:

"Oh! This is General Vinton! Well, I must say that I think you generals have treated the ladies of the Red Cross with precious little courtesy. Here we've been waiting thirty-six hours, and not a soul has come near us or shown us where to go or told us what to do, while everybody else aboard is looked after at once."

"It is a matter entirely out of my jurisdiction, madame," answered the general with grave and distant dignity. "In fact, I knew nothing of the arrival of any such party until, at the commanding general's this morning, your vice-president—is it?—was endeavoring to—"

"Our vice-president, sir," interposed the lady promptly, "is in San Francisco, attending to her proper functions. The person you saw is not recognized by the Red Cross at all, nor by any one in authority that *I* know of."

General Vinton reddened. A soldier, accustomed to the "courtesies indispensable among military men," ill brooks it that a stranger and a woman should take him to task for matters beyond his knowledge or control.

"You will pardon me if in my ignorance of the matter I fancied the lady in question to be a representative of your order, and for suggesting that the chief surgeon is the official to whom you should address your complaint—and rebukes. Good-morning, madame. Miss Ray," he continued, as he quickly turned and led that young lady away, "two of my staff desire to be presented. May I have the pleasure?"

There was no mistaking the general's disapprobation of the official head of the sisterhood as represented on the Sacramento. Though he and his officers remained aboard an hour, not once again would he look towards Dr. Wells or seem to see any of the party but Miss Ray,—this, too, despite the fact that she tried to explain matters and pour oil on such troubled waters.

Captain Butt sent up champagne to the distinguished party, and Miss Ray begged to be excused and slipped away to her stateroom, only to be instantly recalled by other cards— Colonel and Mrs. Brent, other old friends of her father and mother. She remembered them well, and remembered having heard how Mrs. Brent had braved all opposition and had started for Hong Kong the day after the colonel steamed for Manila; and their coming with most hospitable intent only added to the poor girl's perplexities, for they showered welcomes upon her and bade her get her luggage up at once. They had come to take her to their own roof. They had secured such a quaint, roomy house in Ermita right near the bay shore, and looking right out on the Luneta and the parade grounds.

They stormed at her plea that she must not leave her companions. They bade her send for Miss Porter, and included her in their warm-hearted invitation; but by the time Maidie was able to get a word in edgewise on her own account, and begged them to come and meet Mrs. Dr. Wells and the Red Cross sisterhood, they demurred.

The general, in Marion's brief absence, had expressed his opinion of that official head, and the Brents had evidently accepted his views. Then Vinton and his officers loudly begged Mrs. Brent to play chaperon and persuade Miss Ray and Miss Porter to accompany them in their fine white launch on a visit to the admiral on the flag-ship, and said nothing about others of the order.

The idea of seeing Dewey on his own deck and being shown all over the Olympia! Why, it was glorious! But Miss Ray faltered her refusal, even against Miss Porter's imploring eyes. Then Stuyvesant declared he didn't feel up to it.

The general went off to the fleet and the Brents back to shore without the girls. But in the course of the afternoon four more officers came to tender their services to "Billy Ray's daughter," and none, not even a hospital steward, came to do aught for the Red Cross, and by sundown Maidie Ray had every assurance that the most popular girl at that moment in Manila army circles was the least popular aboard the Sacramento, and Kate Porter cried herself to sleep after an out-and-out squabble with two of the Band, and the emphatic assertion that if she were Marion Ray she would cut them all dead and go live with her friends ashore.

But when the morrow came was it to be wondered at that Miss Ray had developed a high fever? Was it not characteristic that before noon, from the official head down, from Dr. Wells to Dottie Fellows, the most diminutive of the party, there lived not a woman of their number who was not eager in tender of services and in desire to be at the sufferer's bedside? Was it not manlike that Stuyvesant, who had shunned the sisterhood for days, now sought the very women he had scorned, and begged for tidings of the girl he loved?

CHAPTER XII

October had come and the rainy season was going, but still the heat of the mid-day sun drove everybody within doors except the irrepressible Yankee soldiery, released "on pass" from routine duty at inner barracks or outer picket line, and wandering about this strange, old-world metropolis of the Philippines, reckless of time or temperature in their determination to see everything there was to be seen about the whilom stronghold of "the Dons" in Asiatic waters.

Along the narrow sidewalks of the Escolta, already bordered by American signs—and saloons,—and rendered even more than usually precarious by American drinks, the blue-shirted boys wandered, open-eyed, marvelling much to find 'twixt twelve and two the shutters up in all the shops not conducted, as were the bars, on the American plan, while from some, still more Oriental, the sun and the shopper both were excluded four full hours, beginning at eleven.

All over the massive, antiquated fortifications of Old Manila into the tortuous mazes of the northern districts, through the crowded Chinese quarter, foul and ill savored, the teeming suburbs of the native Tagals, humble yet cleanly; along the broad, shaded avenues, bordered by stately old Spanish mansions, many of them still occupied by their Castilian owners, the Yankee invaders wandered at will, brimful of curiosity and good nature, eager to gather in acquaintance, information, and bric-a-brac, making themselves perfectly at home, filling the souls of the late lords of the soil with disdain, and those of the natives with wonderment through their lavish, jovial, free and easy ways. Within a month from the time Merritt's little division had marched into the city, Manila was as well known to most of those far-Western volunteers as the streets of their own home villages, and, when once the paymaster had distributed his funds among them and, at the rate of ten cents off on every dollar, they had swapped their sound American coin for "soft" Mexican or Spanish *pesos*, the prodigality with which they scattered their wealth among their dusky friends and admirers evoked the blessings of the church (which was not slow to levy on the beneficiaries), the curses of the sons of Spain, who had generally robbed and never given, and, at first, the almost superstitious awe of the Tagals, who, having never heard of such a thing before, dreaded some deep-laid scheme for their despoilment. But this species of dread lived but a few short weeks, and, before next payday, was as far gone as the money of the Americanos.

Those were blithe days in Manila as the autumn came on and the insurrection was still in the far future. There were fine bands among the Yankee regiments that played afternoon and evening in the kiosk on the Luneta, and every household possessed of an open carriage, or the means of hiring one, appeared regularly each day as the sun sank to the westward sea, and after making swift yet solemn circuit of the Anda monument at the Pasig end of the Paseo de Santa Lucia, returned to the Luneta proper, and wedged in among the closely packed vehicles that covered the broad, smooth driveways on both sides of the esplanade and for some hundred yards each way north and south of the band-stand. Along the shaded and gravelled walks that bordered the Paseo, within short pistol-shot of the grim bastions beyond the green *glacis* and even greener moat, many dark-haired, dark-eyed daughters of Spain, leaving their carriages and, guarded by faithful duenna, strolled slowly up and down, exchanging furtive signal of hand or kerchief with some gallant among the throngs of captive soldiery that swarmed towards sunset on the parapet. Swarthy, black-browed Spanish officers in cool summer uniform and in parties of three or four lined the roadway, or wandered up and down in search of some distraction to the deadly *ennui* of their lives now that their soldier occupation was gone, vouchsafing neither glance nor salutation to their Yankee conquerors, no matter what the rank, until the wives and daughters of American officers began to arrive and appear upon the scene, when the disdain of both sexes speedily gave way to obvious, if reluctant, curiosity.

South of the walls and outworks of Old Manila and east of the Luneta lay a broad, open level, bounded on the south by the suburb of Ermita, and in the midst of the long row of Spanish-built houses extending from the battery of huge Krupps at the bay-side, almost over to the diagonal avenue of the Nozaleda, stood the very cosey, finely furnished house which had been hired as quarters for Colonel Brent, high dignitary on the department staff.

Its lower story of cut stone was pierced by the arched drive-way through which carriages entered to the *patio* or inner court, and, as in the tenets of Madrid the Queen of Spain is possessed of no personal means of locomotion, so possibly to no Spanish dame of high degree may be attributed the desire, even though she have the power, to walk.

No other portal, therefore, either for entrance or exit, could be found at the front. Massive doors of dark, heavy wood from the Luzon forests, strapped with iron, swung on huge hinges that, unless well oiled, defied the efforts of unmuscular mankind. A narrow panel opening in one of these doors, two feet above the ground and on little hinges of its own, gave means of passage to household servants and, when pressed for time, to such of their superiors as would condescend to step high and stoop low.

To the right and left of the main entrance were store-rooms, servants' rooms, and carriage-room, and opposite the latter, towards the rear, the broad stairway that, turning upon itself, led to the living-rooms on the upper floor—the broad salon at the head of the stairs being utilized as a dining-room on state occasions, and its northward end as the parlor. Opening from the sides of the salon, front and rear, were four large, roomy, high-ceilinged chambers.

Overlooking and partially overhanging the street and extending the length of the house was a wide enclosed veranda, well supplied with tables, lounging-chairs, and couches of bamboo and wicker, its floor covered here and there with Indian rugs, its surrounding waist-high railing fitted with parallel grooves in which slid easily the frames of the windows of translucent shells, set in little four-inch squares, or the dark-green blinds that excluded the light and glare of mid-day.

With both thrown back there spread an unobstructed view of the parade-ground even to the edge of the distant *glacis*, and here it was the household sat to watch the military cere-monies, to receive their guests, and to read or doze through-out the drowsier hours of the day. "Campo de Bagumbayan" was what the natives called that martial flat in the strange barbaric tongue that delights in "igs" and "ags," in "ings" and "angs," even to repetition and repletion.

And here one soft, sensuous October afternoon, with a light breeze from the bay tempering the heat of the slanting sunshine, reclining in a broad bamboo easy-chair sat Maidie Ray, now quite convalescent, yet not yet restored to her old-time vigorous health.

Her hostess, the colonel's amiable wife, was busy on the back gallery leading to the kitchen, deep in counsel with her Filipino major-domo and her Chinese cook, servitors who had been well trained and really needed no instruction, and for that matter got but little, for Mrs. Brent's knowledge of the Spanish tongue was even less than her command of "Pidgin" English. Nevertheless, neither Ignacio nor Sing Suey would fail to nod in the one case or smile broadly in the other in assent to her every proposition,—it being one of the articles of their domestic faith that peace and happiness, truth and justice, religion and piety, could best be promoted throughout the establishment by never seeming to differ with the lady of the house. To all outward appearances, therefore, and for the first few weeks, at least, housekeeping in the Philippines seemed something almost idyllic, and Mrs. Brent was in ecstasies over the remarkable virtues of Spanish-trained servants.

There had been anxious days during Maidie's illness. The Sacramento had been ordered away, and the little patient had to be brought ashore. But the chief quartermaster sent his especial steam-launch for "Billy Ray's daughter," the chief surgeon, the best ambulance and team to meet her at the landing; a squad of Sandy's troopers bore her reclining-chair over the side into the launch, out of the launch to the waiting ambulance, and out of the ambulance upstairs into the airy room set apart for her, and, with Mrs. Brent and Miss Porter, Sandy and the most devoted of army doctors to bear her company and keep the fans going, Maidie's progress had been rather in the nature of a triumph.

So at least it had seemed to the austere vice-president of the

Patriotic Daughters of America, who, as it happened, looked on in severe disapproval. She had asked for that very ambulance that very day to enable her to make the rounds of regimental hospitals in the outlying suburbs, and had been politely but positively refused.

By that time, it seems, this most energetic woman had succeeded in alienating all others in authority at corps head-quarters, to the end that the commanding general declined to grant her further audience, the surgeon-general had given orders that she be not admitted to his inner office, the deputy surgeon-general had asked for a sentry to keep her off his premises, the sentries at the First and Second Reserve Hospital had instructions to tell her, also politely but positively, that she could not be admitted except in visiting hours, when the surgeon, a steward, or—and here was "the most unkindest cut of all"—some of the triumphant Red Cross could receive and attend to her, for at last the symbol of Geneva had gained full recognition. At last Dr. Wells and the sisterhood were on duty, comfortably housed, cordially welcomed, and presumably happy.

But Miss Perkins was not. She had come to Manila full of high purpose as the self-styled, accredited representative of any quantity of good Americans, actuated by motives, no doubt, of purest patriotism. The nation was full of it,—of men who wanted to be officers, of women who wanted to be officials, many of whom succeeded only in becoming officious. There were not staff or line positions enough to provide for a hundredth part of the men, or societies and "orders" sufficient to cater to the ambitions of a tenth part of the women. The great Red Cross gave abundant employment for thousands of gentle and willing hands, but limited the number of directing heads, and Miss Perkins and others of the Jellaby stamp were born, as they thought, not to follow but to lead. Balked in their ambitious designs to become prominent in that noble national association, women possessed of the unlimited assurance of Miss Perkins started what might be termed an anti-crusade, with the result that in scores of quiet country towns, as well as in the cities of the East and Middle West, many subscriptions were easily gained, and hundreds of honest, earnest women were rewarded with paper scrolls setting forth that they were named as Sisters of the American Soldier, Patriotic Daughters of America, or Ministering Angels of the Camp and Cot. Shades of Florence Nightingale and Clara Barton! the very voice of such self-appointed angels as Miss Perkins was enough to set the nerves of strong men on edge and to drive fever patients to madness! Even the Red Cross could not always be sure of its selection. It did prevent the sending to Manila of certain undesirable applicants, but it could not prevent the going of Miss Perkins at the expense of the deluded, on ships that were common carriers, even though she were a common scold. There she was, portentous as the British Female portrayed by Thackeray. Backed by apparently abundant means and obviously indomitable "gall," she counted on carrying all before her by sheer force of her powers of self-assertion and the name of the Patriotic Daughters of America. But the commanding general was the most impassive of men, gifted with a keen though little suspected sense of humor, and no little judgment in estimating motive and character. He actually enjoyed the first call made by Miss Perkins, suggested her coming again on the morrow, and summoned his chief surgeon and his provost marshal, another keen humorist, to be present at the interview. It has been asserted that this triumvirate went so far as to encourage the lady to even wilder flights of assertion. We have her own word for it that then and there she was promised as offices three big rooms in the Palace,— the Ayuntamiento,—six clerks, and a private secretary, but an impartial witness avows that the sole basis for this was a question propounded to the provost marshal by the chief surgeon as to whether the chief quartermaster or the chief engineer should be called on to vacate the rooms assigned to them as officers in order that the P. D. A. might be properly recognized and quartered, to which the response was made with unflinching gravity that something certainly should be vacated "P. D. Q." if it took all his clerical force to effect it, but this was *sotto voce*, so to speak, and presumably unheard by the general commanding. It was gall of another kind, and wormwood, after these first few flattering receptions, to be greeted thereafter only by aides-de-camp or a military secretary; then to be told by the chief surgeon that, under instructions from Washington, only those nurses and attendants recognized and employed by the general government could be permitted to occupy quarters or walk the wards about the hospitals. It was bitter to find her criticisms and suggestions set at naught by "impudent young quacks," as she called the delighted doctors of the reserve hospitals, to see the sisterhood of the Red Cross presently clothed with the purple of authority as well as white caps and aprons, while she and, through her, the P. D. A.'s were denied the privilege of stirring up the patients and overhauling the storerooms. Then in her wrath Miss Perkins unbosomed herself to the press correspondents, a few of whom, seeking sensation, as demanded by their papers, took her seriously and told tremendous tales of the brutal neglect of our sick and wounded boys in hospital, of doctors and nurses in wild debauch on the choice wines and liquors sent for the sole use of the sick and wounded by such patriotic societies as the P. D. A.'s, and hinting at other and worse debaucheries (which she blushed to name), and involved in which were prominent officers and favorite members of a rival society "which shall be as nameless as it is shameless." All this had Miss Perkins accomplished within the first eight days of her sojourn, and by way of Hong-Kong the unexpurgated edition of her romance, thrown out by the conscienceless censor at headquarters, eventually found its way to the United States. It was while in this uncharitable frame of mind that Miss Perkins caught sight of the little procession up the Santa Lucia when Maidie was transferred from ship to shore, and the refusal of the best looking of the "impudent young quacks" to permit her to see his patient that afternoon augmented her sense of indignity and wrong. Miss Ray herself went down in the black book of the P. D. A.'s forthwith.

But all this time the officials remained in blissful ignorance of the tremendous nature of the charges laid at their door by this much injured woman, and Maidie Ray, while duly informed of the frequent calls and kind inquiries of many an officer, and permitted of late to welcome Sandy for little talks, had been mercifully spared the infliction of the personal visitation thrice attempted by her fellow-traveller on the train. That awful voice, however, uplifted, as was the habit of the vice-president when aroused, could not fail to reach the sick-room, and when convalescence came and Miss Perkins came not, Maidie made inquiries both of Dr. Frank and of her hostess. Frank showed his handsome teeth and smiled, but Mrs. Brent showed fight. "I won't have such a creature within my doors!" said she. "I don't believe you were ever intimate friends, and that she nursed and cared for you in the cars when you were suffering from shock and fright because of a fire. That's what she says though. What was it, Maidie? Was it there Mr. Stuyvesant got that burn on his face?—and lost his eyebrows?"

And then it transpired that Mr. Stuyvesant had been a frequent and assiduous caller for a whole fortnight, driving thither almost every evening.

But Maidie was oddly silent as to the episode of the fire on the train. She laughed a little about Miss Perkins and her pretensions, but to the disappointment of her hostess could not be drawn into talk about that tall, handsome New Yorker.

And what seemed strange to Mrs. Brent was that now, when Maidie could sit up a few hours each day and see certain among the officers' wives, arriving by almost every steamer from the States, and have happy chats with Sandy every time he could come galloping in from Paco, and was taking delight in watching the parades and reviews on the Bagumbayan, and listening to the evening music of the band, Stuyvesant had ceased to call.

Had Maidie noticed it? Mrs. Brent wondered, as, coming in from her conference with the House of Commons, she stood a moment at the door-way gazing at the girl, whose book had fallen to the floor and whose dark eyes, under their veiling lids were looking far out across the field to the walls and church towers of Old Manila.

It was almost sunset. There was the usual throng of carriages along the Luneta and a great regiment of volunteers, formed in line of platoon columns, was drawn up on the "Campo" directly in front of the house. Sandy had spent his allotted half hour by his sister's side, and, remounting, had cantered out to see the parade. Miss Perkins had declared on the occasion of her third fruitless call that not until Miss Ray sent for her would she again submit herself to be snubbed. So there seemed no immediate danger of her reappearance, and yet Mrs. Brent had given Ignacio orders to open only the panel door when the gate bell clanged, and to refuse admission, even to the drive-way, to a certain importunate caller besides Miss Perkins.

Three days previous there had presented himself a young man in the white dress of the tropics and a hat of fine Manila straw, a young man who would not send up his card, but in very Mexican Spanish asked for Miss Ray. Ignacio sent a boy for Mrs. Brent, who came down to reconnoitre, and the youth reiterated his request.

"An old friend" was all he would say in response to her demand for his name and purpose. She put him off, saying Miss Ray was still too far from well to see anybody, bade him call next day when Dr. Frank and her husband, she knew, would probably be there, duly notified them, and Frank met and received the caller when he came and sent him away in short order.

"The man is a crank," said he, "and I shall have him watched." The colonel asked that one or two of the soldier police guard should be sent to the house to look after the stranger. A corporal came from the company barrack around on the Calle Real, and it was after nightfall when next the "old friend" rang the bell and was permitted by Ignacio to enter.

But the instant the corporal started forward to look at him the caller bounded back into outer darkness. He was tall, sinewy, speedy, and had a twenty-yard start before the little guardsman, stout and burly, could squeeze into the street. Then the latter's shouts up the San Luis only served to startle the sentries, to spur the runner, and to excite and agitate Maidie.

Dr. Frank was disgusted when he tried her pulse and temperature half an hour later and said things to the corporal not strictly authorized by the regulations. The episode was unfortunate, yet might soon have been forgotten but for one hapless circumstance. Despite her announcement, something had overcome Miss Perkins's sense of injury, for she had stepped from a carriage directly in front of the house at the moment of the occurrence, was a witness to all that took place, and the first one to extract from the corporal his version of the affair and his theory as to what lay behind it. In another moment she was driving away towards the Nozaleda, the direction taken by the fugitive, fast as her coachman could whip his ponies, the original purpose of her call abandoned.

As in duty bound, both Mrs. Brent and Dr. Frank had told Sandy of this odd affair. Mrs. Brent described the stranger as tall, slender, sallow, with big cavernous dark eyes that had a wild look to them, and a scraggly, fuzzy beard all over his face, as though he hadn't shaved for long weeks. His hands—of course, she had particularly noticed his hands; what woman doesn't notice such things?—were slim and white. He had the look of a man who had been long in hospital; was probably a recently discharged patient, perhaps one of the many men just now getting their home orders from Washington.

"Somebody who served under your father, perhaps," said Mrs. Brent soothingly to Marion, "and thought he ought to see you."

"Somebody who had not been a soldier at all," said she to Sandy. "He had neither the look nor the manner of one." And Sandy marvelled a bit and decided to be on guard.

"Maidie," he had said that afternoon, before riding away, "when you get out next week we must take up pistol practice again. You beat me at Leavenworth, but you can't do it now. Got your gun—anywhere?—the one Dad gave you?" And Dad or Daddy in the Ray household was the "lovingest" of titles.

Maidie turned a languid head on her pillow. "In the upper drawer of the cabinet in my room, I think," said she. "I remember Mrs. Brent's examining it."

Sandy went in search, and presently returned with the prize, a short, big-barrelled, powerful little weapon of the bull-dog type, sending a bullet like that of a Derringer, hot and hard, warranted to shock and stop an ox at ten yards, but miss a barn at over twenty: a woman's weapon for defence of her life, not a target pistol, and Sandy twirled the shining cylinder approvingly. It was a gleaming toy, with its ivory stock and nickeled steel.

"Every chamber crammed," said Sandy, "and sure to knock spots out of anything from a mad dog to an elephant, provided it hits. Best keep it by you at night, Maidie. These natives are marvellous sneak-thieves. They go all through these ramshackle upper stories like so many ghosts. No one can hear them."

Then, when he took his leave, the pistol remained there lying on the table, and Frank, coming in to see his most interesting patient just as the band was trooping back to its post on the right of the long line, picked it up and examined it, muzzle uppermost, with professional approbation.

"Yours I see, Miss Ray;—and from your father. A man hit by one of these," he continued musingly, and fingering the fat leaden bullets, "would drop in his tracks. You keep it by you?—always?"

"I? No!" laughed Maidie. "I'm eager to get to my work,—healing—not giving—gunshot wounds."

"You will have abundant time, my dear young lady," said the doctor slowly, as he carefully replaced the weapon on the table by her side, "and—opportunity, if I read the signs aright, and we must get you thoroughly well before you begin. Ah! What's that? What's the matter over there?" he lazily asked. It was a fad of the doctor's never to permit himself to show the least haste or excitement.

A small opera-glass stood on the sill, and, calmly adjusting it as he peered, Frank had picked it up and levelled it towards the front and centre of the line just back of where the colonel commanding sat in saddle. A lively scuffle and commotion had suddenly begun among the groups of spectators. Miss Ray's reclining-chair was so placed that by merely raising her head she could look out over the field. Mrs. Brent ran to where the colonel's field-glasses hung in their leathern case and joined the doctor at the gallery rail.

Three pairs of eyes were gazing fixedly at the point of disturbance, already the centre of a surging crowd of soldiers off duty, oblivious now to the fact that the band was playing the "Star-Spangled Banner," and they ought to be standing at attention, hats off, and facing the flag as it came floating slowly to earth on the distant ramparts of the old city.

Disdainful of outside attractions, the adjutant came stalking out to the front as the strain ceased, and his shrill voice was heard turning over the parade to his commander. Then the surging group seemed to begin to dissolve, many following a little knot of men carrying on their shoulders an apparently inanimate form. They moved in the direction of the old botanical garden, towards the Estado Mayor, and so absorbed were the three in trying to fathom the cause of the excitement that they were deaf to Ignacio's announcement. A tall, handsome, most distinguished-looking young officer stood at the wide door-way, dressed *cap-a-pie* in snowy white, and not until, after a moment's hesitation, he stepped within the room and was almost upon them, did Miss Ray turn and see him.

"Why, Mr. Stuyvesant!" was all she said; but the tone was enough. Mrs. Brent and the doctor dropped the glasses and whirled about. Both instantly noted the access of color. It had not all disappeared by any means, though the doctor had, when, ten minutes later, Colonel Brent came in.

At the moment of his entrance, Stuyvesant, seated close to Marion's reclining-chair, was, with all the doctor's caution and curiosity, examining her revolver. "Rather bulky for a pocket-pistol," he remarked, as, muzzle downward, he essayed its insertion in the gaping orifice at the right hip of his Manila-made, flapping white trousers. It slipped in without a hitch.

"What was the trouble out there a while ago?" asked the lady of the house of her liege lord. "You saw it, I suppose?"

"Nothing much. Man had a fit, and it took four men to hold him. Maidie, look here. Captain Kress handed this to me— said they picked it up just back of where the colonel stood at parade. Is he another mash?"

Marion took the envelope from the outstretched hand, drew forth a little *carte-de-visite*, on which was the vignette portrait of her own face, gave one quick glance, and dropped back on the pillow. All the bright color fled. The picture fell to the floor. "Can you—find Sandy?" was all she could say, as, with imploring eyes, she gazed into honest Brent's astonished face.

"I can, at once," said Stuyvesant, who had risen from his chair at the colonel's remark. With quick bend he picked up the little card, placed it face downward on the table by her side, never so much as giving one glance at the portrait, and noiselessly left the room.

CHAPTER XIII

Like many another man's that summer and autumn of '98, Mr. Gerard Stuyvesant's one overwhelming ambition had been to get on to Manila. The enforced sojourn at Honolulu had been, therefore, a bitter trial. He had reached at last the objective point of his soldier desires, and with all his heart now wished himself back on the Sacramento with one, at least,—or was it at most?—of the Sacramento's passengers. The voyage had done much to speed his recovery. The cordial greeting extended by his general and comrade officers had gladdened his heart. Pleasant quarters on the breezy bay shore, daily drives, and, presently, gentle exercise in saddle had still further benefited him.

He had every assurance that Marion Ray's illness was not of an alarming nature, and that, soon as the fever had run its course, her convalescence would be rapid. He was measurably happy in the privilege of calling every day to ask for her, but speedily realized the poverty of Oriental marts in the means wherewith to convey to the fair patient some tangible token of his constant devotion. Where were the glorious roses, the fragrant, delicate violets, the heaping baskets of cool, luscious, tempting grapes, pears, and peaches with which from Saco to Seattle, from the Sault de Sainte Marie to Southwest Pass, in any city outside of Alaska in the three million square miles of his own native land, he could have laid siege to her temporary retreat? Ransack the city as he might,—market, shops, and gardens,—hardly a flower could he find worthy her acceptance—a garish, red-headed hybrid twixt poppy and tulip and some inodorous waxen shoots that looked like decrepit hyacinths and smelled like nothing, representing the stock in trade at that season of the few flower-stands about Manila. As for fruit, some stunted sugar bananas about the size of a shoehorn and a few diminutive China oranges proved the extent of the weekly exhibit along the Escolta. Once, La Extremena displayed a keg of Malaga grapes duly powdered with cork, and several pounds of these did Stuyvesant levy upon forthwith, and, after being duly immersed in water and cooled in the ice-chest, send them in dainty basket by a white-robed lackey, with an unimpeachable card bearing the legend "Mr. Gerard Stuyvesant, One-Hundred-and-Sixth New York Infantry Volunteers," and much were they admired on arrival, but that was in the earlier days of Maidie's convalescence, and Dr. Frank shook his head. Grape-seeds were "perilous stuff," and Mrs. Brent knew they would not last until Maidie was well enough to enjoy them, and so—they did not.

Military duty for the staff was not exacting about Manila in the autumn days. It was the intermission. The Spanish war was over; the Filipino yet to come. There was abundant time for "love and sighing," and Stuyvesant did both, for there was no question the poor fellow had found his fate, and yet thought it trembling in the balance. Not one look or word of hers for him could Stuyvesant recall that was more winsome and kind than those bestowed on other men. Indeed, had he not seen with jealous eyes with what beaming cordiality and delight she had met and welcomed one or two young gallants, who, having been comrades of Sandy in "the Corps" at the Point, had found means to get out to the Sacramento, obviously to see her, just before that untimely illness claimed her for its own? Had he not heard his general, his fellow staff officers, speaking enthusiastically of her beauty and fascinations and their destructive effects in various quarters? Had he not been compelled in silence to listen again and in detail to the story of old Sam Martindale's nephew?—Sam Martingale, the cavalry called him—"Martinet Martindale" he was dubbed by the "doughboys"—that conscientious, dutiful, and therefore none too popular veteran, whose sister's children much more than supplied the lack of his own.

Farquhar of the cavalry, scion of a Philadelphia family well known to the Stuyvesants of Gotham and "trotting in the same class," had come over from department head-quarters, where he had a billet as engineer officer, to call on Stuyvesant and to cheer him up and contribute to his convalescence, and did so after the manner of men, by talking on all manner of topics for nearly an hour and winding up by a dissertation on Billy Ray's pretty daughter and "Wally" Foster's infatuation. Farquhar said it was the general belief that Maidie liked Wally mighty well and would marry him were he only in the army. And Stuyvesant wondered how it was, in all the years he had known Farquhar and envied him his being a West Pointer and in the cavalry, he had never really discovered what a bore, what a wearisome ass, Farquhar could be.

Then just as Miss Ray was reported sitting up and soon to be able to "see her friends,"—with what smiling significance did Mrs. Brent so assure him!—what should Stuyvesant's general do but select Stuyvesant himself to go on a voyage of discovery to Iloilo and beyond. The commanding general wanted a competent officer who spoke Spanish to make a certain line of investigation. He consulted Vinton. Vinton thought another voyage the very thing for Stuyvesant, and so suggested his name.

It sent the luckless Gothamite away just at the time of all others he most wished to remain. When he returned, within a dozen days, the first thing was to submit his written report, already prepared aboard ship. The next was to report himself in person at Colonel Brent's, to be asked into the presence of the girl he loved and longed to see, and, as has been told, ushered out almost immediately, self-detailed, in search of Sandy.

He had found the lad easily enough, but not so the man with the fit, whom, for reasons of his own and from what he had seen and heard, Stuyvesant was most anxious to overtake. His carriage whirled him rapidly past the parade-ground and over to the First Reserve Hospital, whither he thought the victim had been borne, but no civilian, with or without fits, had recently been admitted.

Inquiry among convalescent patients and soldiers along the road without resulted at last in his finding one of the party that carried the stricken man from the field. He had come to, said the volunteer, before they had gone quarter of a mile, had soused his head in water at a hydrant, rested a minute, offered them a quarter for their trouble, buttoned up the light coat that had been torn open in his struggle, and nervously but positively declared himself all right and vastly obliged, had then hailed a passing *carromatta*, and been whisked away across the moat and drawbridge into the old city. There all trace was lost of him.

Baffled and troubled, Stuyvesant ordered his coachman to take him to the Luneta. The crowd had disappeared. The carriages were nearly all departed. The lights were twinkling here and there all over the placid bay. It was still nearly an hour to dinner-time at the general's mess, and he wished to be alone to think over matters, to hear the soothing plash and murmur of the little waves, and Stuyvesant vowed in his wrath and vexation that Satan himself must be managing his affairs, for, over and above the longed-for melody of the rhythmic waters, he was hailed by the buzz-saw stridencies of Miss Perkins, whose first words gave the lie to themselves.

"I'm all out of breath, and so het up runnin' after you I can't talk, but I was just bound to see you, an' I've been to your house so often the soldiers laugh at me. Those young men haven't any sense of decency or respect, but I'll teach 'em, and you see they'll sing another song. Where can we sit down?" continued the lady, her words chasing each other's heels in her breathless haste. "These lazy, worthless Spanish officers take every seat along here. Why, here! your carriage will do, an' I've got a thousand things to say!" ("Heaven be merciful," groaned Stuyvesant to himself.) "I saw you driving, and I told my cabman to catch you if he had to flog the hide off his horse. Come, aren't you—don't you want to sit down? I do, anyhow! There's no comfort in my cab. Here, I'll dismiss it now. You can just drop me on the way home, you know. I'm living down the Calle Real a few blocks this side of you. All the soldiers know me, and if *they* had *their* say it wouldn't be the stuck-up Red Cross that's flirting with doctors and living high on the dainties our folks sent over. The *boys* are all right. It's your generals that have ignored the P. D. A.'s, and I'll show 'em presently what a miss they've made. Wait till the papers get the letters I have written. But, say—"("And this is the woman I thought might be literary!" moaned Stuyvesant as he meekly followed to the little open carriage and, with a shiver, assisted his angular visitor to a seat.)

"A Key!" she shouted, "A Key, Cochero! No quiere mas hoy. Manana! Ocho! Sabe, Cochero? Ocho! Now don't chewbe— What's late in their lingo, anyhow? 'Tisn't tardy, I know; that's afternoon. Tardeeo? Thank you. Now—well, just sit down, first, lieutenant. You see *we* know how to address officers by their titles, if the Red Cross don't. I'd teach 'em to Mister me if I was an officer. Now, what I want to see you about first is this. Your general has put me off one way or another every time I've called this last two weeks. I've always treated him politely, but for some reason he'll never see me now, and yet they almost ran after me at first. Now, you can fix it easy enough, and you do it and you won't regret it. I only want him to listen to me three minutes, and that's little enough for anybody to ask. You do it, and I can do a good deal more for you than you think for, an' I will do it, too, if certain people don't treat me better. It's something you'll thank me for mightily later on if you don't now. I've had my eyes open, lieutenant, an' I see things an' I hear things an' I know things you mighty little suspect."

"Pardon me, Miss Perkins," interposed Stuyvesant at this juncture, his nerves fairly twitching under the strain. "Let us get at the matters on which you wish to speak to me. Malate, Cochero!" he called to the pygmy Filipino on the box. "I am greatly pressed for time," he added, as the carriage whirled away, the hoofs of the pony team flying like shuttles the instant the little scamps were headed homeward.

"Well, what I want mostly is to see the general. He's got influence with General Drayton and I know it, and these Red Cross people have poisoned his ears. Everybody's ears seem to be just now against me and I can get no hearing whatever. Everything was all right at first; everything was promised me, and then, first one and then another, they all backed out, and I want to know why—I'm bound to know why, and they'd better come to me and make their peace now than wait until the papers and the P. D. A.'s get after 'em, as they will,—you hear my words now,—they *will* do just as soon as my letters reach the States. *You're* all right enough. I've told them how you helped with those poor boys of mine aboard the train. Bad way they'd been in if we hadn't been there, you and I. Why, I just canvassed that train till I got clothes and shoes for every one of those poor burned-out fellows, but there wouldn't anybody else have done it. And nursing?—you ought to have seen those boys come to thank me the day I went out to the Presidio, an' most cried—some of them did;—said their own mothers couldn't have done more, and they'd do anything for me now. But when I went out to their camp at Paco their major just as much as ordered me away, and that little whipper-snapper, Lieutenant Ray, that I could take on my knee and spank—He—Lieutenant Ray—a friend of yours? Well, you may *think* he is, or you may be a friend of *his*, but *I* can tell you right here and now he's no friend, and you'll see he isn't. What's more, I hate to see an honest, high-toned young gentleman just throwing himself away on people that can't appreciate him. I could tell you—"

"Stop, driver!" shouted Stuyvesant, unable longer to control himself. "Miss Perkins," he added, as the little coachman manfully struggled to bring his rushing team to a halt at the curb, "I have a call to make and am late. Tell my coachman where to take you and send him back to this corner. Good-night, madam," and, gritting his teeth, out he sprang to the sidewalk.

It happened to be directly in front of one of those native resorts where, day and night, by dozens the swarthy little brown men gather about a billiard-table with its centre ornament of boxwood pins, betting on a game resembling the Yankee "pin pool" in everything but the possibility of fair play. Hovering about the entrance or on the outskirts of the swarm of men and boys, a dozen native women, some with babies in their arms and nearly all with cigars between their teeth, stood watching the play with absorbing interest, and a score of dusky, pot-bellied children from two to twelve years of age sprawled about the premises, as much at home as the keeper of the place.

The lamps had been lighted but a few minutes and the game was in full blast. Some stalwart soldiers, regulars from the Cuartel de Malate from down the street or the nipa barracks of the Dakotas and Idahos, were curiously studying the scene, making jovial and unstinted comment after their fearless democratic fashion, but sagely abstaining from trying their luck and not so sagely sampling the sizzling soda drinks held forth to them by tempting hands. Liquor the vendors dare not proffer,—the provost marshal's people had forbidden that,—and only at the licensed bars in town or by bribery and stealth in the outlying suburbs could the natives dispose of the villainous "bino" with which at times the unwary and unaccustomed American was overcome.

Three or four men in civilian dress, that somehow smacked of the sea, as did their muttered, low-toned talk, huddled together at the corner post, furtively eying the laughing soldiers and occasionally peering up and down the darkened street. It was not the place Stuyvesant would have chosen to leave his carriage, but it was a case of any port in a storm,— anything to escape that awful woman. With one quick spring he was out of the vehicle and into the midst of the group on the narrow sidewalk before he noticed them at all, but not before they saw him. Even as Miss Perkins threw forward a would-be grasping and detaining hand and called him by name, one of the group in civilian dress gave sudden, instant start, sprang round the corner, but, tripping on some obstacle, sprawled full length on the hard stone pavement. Despite the violence of the fall, which wrung from him a fierce curse, the man was up in a second, away, and out of sight in a twinkling.

"Go on!" shouted Stuyvesant impatiently, imperiously, to his coachman, as, never caring what street he took, he too darted around the same corner, and his tall white form vanished on the track of the civilian.

But the sound of the heavy fall, the muttered curse, and the sudden question in the nearest group, "What's wrong with Sackett?" had reached Miss Perkins's ears, for while once more the little team was speeding swiftly away, the strident voice of the lone passenger was uplifted in excited hail to the coachman to stop. And here the Filipino demonstrated to the uttermost that the amenities of civilization were yet undreamed of in his darkened intellect—as between the orders of the man and the demands of the woman he obeyed the former. Deaf, even to that awful voice, he drove furiously on until brought up standing by the bayonets of the patrol in front of the English Club, and in a fury of denunciation and quiver of mingled wrath and excitement, Miss Perkins tumbled out into the arms of an amazed and disgusted sergeant, and demanded that he come at once to arrest a vile thief and deserter.

CHAPTER XIV

That night the sentries all over the suburbs of Ermita and Malate were peering into every dark alleyway and closely scrutinizing every human being nearing their posts. Few and far between were these, for the natives were encouraged to remain indoors after nine o'clock, and the soldiers forbidden to be out. The streets were deserted save by occasional carriage or carromatta bearing army or navy officers, or what were termed the foreign residents—English or German as a rule—from club or calls to their quarters.

"Lights out" sounded early at the barracks of the soldiery, for they were up with the dawn for breakfast that they might be through with their hardest drills before the heat of the day. The "pool rooms," as the big *Americanos* called these "wide open," single-tabled billiard saloons that flourished in almost every block, were required to put up their shutters at nine o'clock, and every discoverable establishment in which gambling had prevailed in other form had long since been closed by a stony-hearted chief of police, whose star was worn on each shoulder rather than the left breast, and who, to the incredulous amaze of Spaniard and Filipino alike, listened unmoved to the pleas of numerous prominent professors of the gambling industry, even when backed by proffers of a thousand a week in gold. That the "*partida de billar*" had not also been suppressed was due to the fact that, like Old Sledge in the Kentucky Court, its exponents established it to be, not a game of chance, but skill, and such, indeed, it proved to every Yankee who put up his money against the bank. With an apparently congenital gift of sleight of hand, developed by years of practice at pitch penny from toddling babyhood to cock-fighting adolescence, the native could so manipulate the tools of his game that no outsider had the faintest "show for his money," while, as against each other, as when Greek met Greek, it became a battle of the giants, a trial of almost superhuman skill. It was the one game left to adult Tagalhood in which he might indulge his all-absorbing and unconquerable passion to play for money. All over town and suburbs wandered countless natives with wondering game-cocks under their arms, suffering for a chance to spur if not to "scrap," for even the national sport had been stopped. Never in all the services in all the churches of Luzon had such virtue been preached as that practised by these heartless, soulless invaders from across the wide Pacific—men who stifled gambling and scorned all bribes. "Your chief of police is no gentleman," declared certain prominent merchants, arrested for smuggling opium, and naturally aggrieved and indignant at such unheard-of treatment. "He did not tell us how much he wanted! He did not even ask us to pay!" Retained in responsible positions in the office of the collector of customs, two Spanish officers of rank were presently found to have embezzled some twelve thousand dollars in some six weeks of opportunity. "But this is outrage! This is scandalous!" quoth they, in righteous wrath on being bidden to disgorge and ordered before a court-martial. "We have nothing but the customary perquisite! It is you who would rob us!" From highest to lowest, in church, in state, in school,—in every place,—there seemed no creed that barred the acquisition of money by any means short of actual robbery of the person. As for thieving from the premises, the Filipino stood unequalled—the champion sneak-thief of the universe.

And the sentries this night, softly lighted by a waning old moon, were on the lookout everywhere among the suburbs for two malefactors distinctly differing in type, yet equally in demand. One, said the descriptions, compiled from the original information of Zenobia Perkins, Spinster; residence 259 Calle Real, Ermita; occupation, Vice-President and Accredited Representative for the Philippine Islands of the Patriotic Daughters of America, and the additional particulars later obtained from Lieutenant Gerard Stuyvesant, aide-de-camp to General Vinton, 595 Calle Real, Malate— one, said the descriptions, was a burly, thick-set, somewhat slouching American, in clothing of the sailor slop-shop variety, a man of five feet six and maybe forty years, though he might be much younger; a coarse-featured, heavy-bearded man, with gray eyes, generally bleary, and one front tooth gone, leaving a gap in the upper jaw next the canine, which was fang-like, yellow, and prominent; a man with harsh voice and surly ways; a man known as Sackett among seamen and certain civilians who probably had made their way to Manila in the hope of picking up an easy living; a man wanted as Murray among soldiers for a deserter, jail-bird, and thief.

The other malefactor was less minutely described. A native five feet eight, perhaps. Very tall for a Tagal, slender, sinewy, and with a tuft of wiry hair and sixteen inches of shirt missing. "For further particulars and the missing sixteen inches, as well as the hair, inquire at Colonel Brent's, Number 199 Calle San Luis, Ermita."

It seems that soon after dark that eventful evening Mrs. Brent and Miss Porter had seen Maidie comfortably bestowed in the big, broad, cane-bottomed bed in her airy room, and had left her to all appearances sleeping placidly towards eight o'clock, and then gone out to dinner. Whatever the cause of her agitation on receiving at Brent's hands the little card photograph of herself, it had subsided after a brief, low-toned conference with Sandy, who quickly came and speedily hastened away, and a later visit from Dr. Frank, whose placid, imperturbable, restful ways were in themselves well-nigh as soothing as the orange-flower water prescribed for her. Even the little night-light, floating in its glass, had been extinguished when the ladies left her.

The room assigned to Marion was at the north-west corner of the house. Its two front windows opened on the wide gallery, that in turn opened out on the Bagumbayan parade. Its west windows, also two in number, were heavily framed. There were sliding blinds to oppose to the westering sun, translucent shells in place of brittle glass to temper, yet admit, the daylight, and hanging curtains that slid easily on their supporting rods and rendered the room dark as could be desired for the siesta hours of the tropic day.

The dinner-table, brightly lighted by lamps hung from hooks securely driven in the upper beams (lath and plaster are unknown in this seismic land), was set on the rear gallery overlooking the *patio*, and here, soon after eight, Brent, his little household, the doctor, and two more guests were cosily chatting and dining, while noiseless native servants hovered about and Maidie Ray presumably slept.

But Maidie was not sleeping. Full of a new anxiety, if not of dread, and needing to think calmly and clearly, she had turned away from her almost too assiduous attendants and closed her eyes upon the world about her. A perplexity, a problem such as never occurred to her as a possibility, one that sorely worried Sandy, as she could plainly see, had suddenly been thrust upon her. Hitherto she had ever had a most devoted mother as her counsellor and friend, but now a time had come when she must think and act for herself.

The little card photograph picked up by the men on the scene of the scuffle at the edge of the Bagumbayan had told its story to her at least and to Sandy. It could only mean that Foster, he who spent whole days and weeks at their New Mexican station to the neglect of his cattle-ranch, he who had 'listed in the cavalry and disappeared—deserted, maybe—at Carquinez, had eluded search, pursuit, inquiry of every kind, and, all ignorant, probably, of the commission obtained for him, had, still secretly, as though realizing his danger, followed her to Manila.

This then must have been the tall stranger who called himself an old friend and would give no name, for it was to Foster, in answer to his most urgent plea,—perhaps touched by his devoted love for her lovely daughter,—that Mrs. Ray had given that little vignette photograph long months before. There, on the back, was the date in her mother's hand, "Fort Averill, New Mexico, February 15, 1898." Well did Marion remember how he had begged her to write her name beneath the picture, and how, for some reason she herself could not describe, she had shrunk from so doing. There had been probably half a dozen pictures of Foster about their quarters at Averill,—photographs in evening dress, in ranch rig, in winter garb, in tennis costume,—but only one had he of Maidie, and that not of her giving.

Now, what could his coming mean? What madness prompted this stealth and secrecy? If innocent of wilful desertion, his proper course was to have reported without delay to the military authorities at San Francisco and told the cause of his disappearance or detention. But he had evidently done nothing of the kind. They would surely have heard of it, and now he was here, still virtually in hiding and possibly in disguise, and one unguarded word of hers might land him a prisoner, a war-time deserter, within the walls of the gloomy carcel in Old Manila.

Sandy she had to tell, and he was overwhelmed with dismay, had galloped to Paco to see his colonel and get leave for "urgent personal and family reasons," as he was to say, to spend forty-eight hours in and about Manila. If a possible thing, Sandy was to trail and find poor Foster, induce him to surrender himself at once, to plead illness, inexperience,— anything,—and throw himself on the mercy of the authorities. Sandy would be back by nine unless something utterly unforeseen detained him at East Paco. Meantime what else could she do?—what could she plan to rescue that reckless, luckless, hare-brained, handsome fellow from the plight into which his misguided, wasted passion had plunged him?

From the veranda the clink of glass and china, the low hum of merry chat, the sound of half-smothered laughter, fell upon the ear and vexed her with its careless jollity. Impatiently she threw herself upon the other—the left—side, and then—sat bolt upright in bed.

Not a breath of air was stirring. The night was so still she could hear the soft tinkle of the ships' bells off the Luneta,— could almost hear the soothing plash of the wavelets on the beach. There was nothing whatever to cause that huge mahogany door to swing upon its well-oiled hinges. She heard them close it when they went out; she saw that it was closed when they were gone, yet, as she turned on her pillow and towards the faint light through the northwest windows, that door was slowly, stealthily turning, until at last, wide open, it interposed between her and the outward light at the front.

Many an evening lately she had lain with hands clasped under the back of her bonny head looking dreamily out through that big open window, across the gallery beyond and the open casements in front, watching the twinkle of the electric lights above the distant ramparts of the old city and the nearer gleam of the brilliant globes that hung aloft along the west edge of the Bagumbayan.

Now one-half of that vista was shut off by the massive door, the other was unobscured, but even as with beating heart, still as a trembling mouse, she sat and gazed, something glided slowly, stealthily, noiselessly between her and those betraying lights, something dark, dim, and human, for the shape was that of a man, a native, as she knew by the stiffly brushed-up hair above the forehead, the loosely falling shirt—a native taller than any of their household servants—a native whose movements were so utterly without sound that Maidie realized on the instant that here was one of Manila's famous veranda-climbing house-thieves, and her first thought was for her revolver. She had left it, totally forgotten, on the little table on the outer gallery.

Even though still weak from her long and serious illness, the brave, army-bred girl was conscious of no sentiment of fear. To cry out was sure to bring about the instant escape of the intruder, whereas to capture him and prevent his getting away with such valuables as he had probably already laid hands on became instantly her whole ambition. The side windows were closed by the sliding blinds. Even if he leaped from them it would be into a narrow court shut in by a ten-foot, spike-topped stone wall. He had chosen the veranda climber's favorite hour, that which found the family at dinner on the back gallery, and the quiet streets well-nigh deserted save by his own skilled and trusted "pals," from whose shoulders he had easily swung himself to the overhanging structure at the front. He would doubtless retire that way the moment he had stowed beneath his loose, flapping *ropas* such items as he deemed of marketable value.

He was even now stealthily moving across the floor to where

her dressing-table stood between the westward windows. The man must have the eyes of a cat to see in the dark, or else personal and previous knowledge of the premises. If she could only slip as noiselessly out by the foot of the bed, interpose between him and the door and that one wide-open window, then scream for help and grab him as he sprang, she might hope to hold him a second or two, and then Brent and Dr. Frank would be upon him.

All her trembling was from excitement: she knew no thought of fear. But strong and steady hands were needed, not the fever-shattered members only just beginning to regain their normal tone. She slid from underneath the soft, light coverlet without a sound. The sturdy yet elastic bottom of platted cane never creaked or complained. She softly pushed outward the fine mosquito netting, gathered her dainty night-robe closely about her slender form, and the next minute her little bare feet were on the polished, hard-wood floor, the massive door barely five short steps away. She cautiously lifted the netting till it cleared her head, and then, crouching low, moved warily towards the dim, vertical slit that told of subdued light in the salon.

There was no creak to those thick, black-wood planks with which Manila mansions are floored. Her outstretched hand had almost reached the knob when her knee collided with a light bamboo bedroom chair. There was instant bamboo rasp and protest, followed by instant vigorous spring across the room, and instant piercing scream from Maidie's lips.

Something dusky white shot before her eyes, something inky black and dusky white was snatched at and seized by those nervous, slender, but determined little hands. Something dropped with clash and clatter on the resounding floor. Something ripped and tore as an agile, slippery, squirming form bounded from her grasp over the casement to the veranda, over the sill into the street, and when Brent and the doctor and the women-folk came rushing in and lamps were brought and Brent went shouting to sentries up and down the San Luis and shots were heard around the nearest corner, Maid Marion, Second, was found crouching upon the cane-bottomed chair that had baffled her plans, half-laughing, half-crying with vexation, but firmly grasping in one hand a tuft of coarse, straight black hair, and in the other a section of Filipino shirt the size of a lady's kerchief—all she had to show of her predatory visitor and to account for the unseemly disturbance they had made.

"Just to think—just to think!" exclaimed Mrs. Brent, with clasping hands, "that this time, when you might most have needed it, Mr. Stuyvesant should have gone off with your pistol!"

CHAPTER XV

But there was little merriment when, five minutes later, the household had taken account of stock and realized the extent of their losses.

Maidie's had evidently been the last room visited. The dressing-table and wardrobe of the opposite chamber—that occupied by Colonel and Mrs. Brent—had been ransacked. The colonel's watch and chain,—too bulky, he said, to be worn at dinner in white uniform,—his Loyal Legion and Army of the Potomac insignia, and some prized though not expensive trinkets of his good wife were gone. Miss Porter's little purse with her modest savings and a brooch that had been her mother's were missing. And with these items the skilled practitioner had made good his escape.

On the floor, just under the window in Maidie's room, lay a keen, double-edged knife. The stumps of two or three matches found in the colonel's apartment and others in Miss Porter's showed that the thief had not feared to make sufficient light for his purpose, and from the floor of Marion's room, close to the bureau, just where it had been dropped when the prowler was alarmed, Miss Porter picked up one of the old-fashioned "phosphors" that ignite noiselessly and burn with but a tiny flame.

Marion's porte-monnaie was in the upper drawer, untouched, and such jewelry as she owned, save two precious rings she always wore, was stored in her father's safe deposit box in the bank at home. The colonel was really the greatest loser and declared it served him right, both provost-marshal and chief of police having warned him to leave nothing "lying around loose."

At sound of the shots on the Calle Nueva, Brent had sallied forth, and, rushing impetuously into the dimly lighted thoroughfare, had narrowly missed losing the top of his head as well as his watch, an excited sentry sending a bullet whizzing into space by way of the colonel's pith helmet, which prompted the doctor to say in his placid and most effective way that more heads had been lost that night than valuables, and one bad shot begat another.

Sentries down towards the barracks, hearing the three or four quick reports, bethought them of the time-honored instructions prescribing that in case of a blaze, which he could not personally extinguish, the sentry should "shout 'Fire!' discharge his piece, and add the number of his post." Sagely reasoning that nothing but a fire could start such a row, or at least that there was sufficient excuse to warrant their having some fun of their own to enliven the dull hours of the night, Numbers 7 and 8 touched off their triggers and yelled "Fire;" 5 and 6, nearer home, followed suit, and in two minutes the bugles were blowing the alarm all over Ermita and Malate, and rollicking young regulars and volunteers by the hundred were tumbling out into the street, all eagerness and rejoicing at the prospect of having a lark with the *Bomberos*, the funny little Manila firemen with their funnier little squirts on wheels.

It was fully half an hour before the officers could "locate" the origin of the alarm and order their companies back to bed, an order most reluctantly obeyed, for by that time the nearest native fire-company was aroused and on the way to the scene. Others could be expected in the course of the night, and the Manila fire department was something that afforded the Yankee soldier unspeakable joy. He hated to lose such an opportunity.

But for all his professional calm, Dr. Frank was by no means pleased with the excitement attending this episode. For an hour or more officers from all over the neighborhood gathered in front of Brent's and had to be told the particulars, "Billy Ray's daughter" being pronounced the heroine everybody expected her to be, while that young lady herself, now that the affair could be called closed, was in a condition bordering on the electric. "Overwrought and nervous," said Miss Porter, "but laughing at the whole business."

What Frank thought he didn't say, but he cut short Sandy's visit to his sister, and suggested that he go down and tell the assemblage under the front gallery that they would better return to whist—or whatever game was in progress when the alarm was given. The colonel could not invite them in as matters stood, and they slowly dispersed, leaving only a senior or two and Lieutenant Stuyvesant to question further, for Stuyvesant, coming from afar and arriving late, was full of anxiety and concern.

Despite his temporary escape, circumstances and the civil authorities (now become decidedly military) had thrown him into still further association with the woman whom he would so gladly have shunned—the importunate Miss Perkins. He had taken a turn round the block—and refuge in the English Club—until he thought her disposed of at home and his carriage returned. He had come across the little equipage, trundling slowly up and down the street in search of him, had dined without appetite and smoked without relish, striving to forget that odious woman's hints and aspersions, aimed evidently at the Rays, and had gone to his own room to write when a corporal appeared with the request from the captain in charge of the police guard of Ermita to step down to the office.

It was much after nine then and the excitement caused by the alarm was about over, the troops going back to barracks and presumably to bed. The captain apologized for calling on him that late in the evening, but told him a man recognized as Murray, deserter from the cavalry, was secreted somewhere in the neighborhood, and it was reported that he, Stuyvesant, could give valuable information concerning him. Stuyvesant could and did, and in the midst of it in came Miss Perkins, flushed, eager, and demanding to know if that villain was yet caught—"and if not, why not?"

Then she caught sight of Stuyvesant and precipitated herself upon him. That man Murray had hatefully deceived her and imposed upon her goodness, she declared. She had done *everything* to help him at the Presidio, and he had promised her a paper signed by all the boys asking that the P. D. A.'s be recognized as the organization the soldiers favored, and showed her a petition he had drawn up and was getting signatures to by the hundreds. That paper would have insured their being recognized by the government instead of those purse-proud Red Cross people, and then he had wickedly deserted, after—after—and Stuyvesant could scarcely keep a straight face—getting fifty dollars from her and a ring that he was going to wear always until he came back from Manila—an officer. Oh, he was a smart one, a smooth one! All that inside of three days after he got to the Presidio, and then was arrested, and then, next thing she knew, he had fled,—petition, money, ring, and all.

Another soldier told her the signatures were bogus. And that very night she recognized him, spite of his beard, and at sight of her he had cut and run. ("Well he might!" thought Stuyvesant.) And then Miss Perkins yielded to the strain of overtaxed nerves and had to be conducted home.

She lived but a block or two away, and it was Stuyvesant who had to play escort. The air, unluckily, revived her, and at the gateway she turned and had this to add to her previous statements.

"You think the Ray people your friends, lieutenant, and I'm not the kind of a woman to see a worthy young man trifled with. You've been going there every day and everybody knows it, and knows that you were sent away to Iloilo in hopes of breaking you of it. That girl's promised in marriage to that young man who's got himself into such a scrape all on her account. He's here—followed her here to marry her, and if he's found he's liable to be shot. Oh, you can believe or not just as you please, but never say I didn't try to give you fair warning. Know? Why, I know much more about what's going on here than your generals do. *I* have friends everywhere among the boys; *they* haven't. Oh, very well, if you won't listen!" (For Stuyvesant had turned away in wrath and exasperation.) "But you'd be wiser if you heard me out. I've *seen* Mr. Foster and had the whole story from his lips. He's been there every day, too, till he was taken sick—"

But Stuyvesant was out of the gate and at last out of hearing, and with a vicious bang to the door, the lady of the P. D. A.'s, so recently victimized by the astute Sackett, retired to the sanctity of her own apartment, marvelling at the infatuation of men.

And yet, though Stuyvesant had angrily striven to silence the woman and had left her in disgust, her words had not failed of certain weight. Again he recalled with jealous pain the obvious indifference with which his approaches had been received. True, no well-bred girl would be more than conventionally civil to a stranger even under the exceptional circumstances of their meeting on the train. True, she was cordial, bright, winsome, and all that when at last he was formally presented; but so she was to everybody. True, they had had many—at least *he* had had many—delightful long interviews on the shaded deck of the Sacramento; but though he would have eagerly welcomed a chance to indulge in sentiment, never once did Marion encourage such a move. On the contrary, he recalled with something akin to bitterness that when his voice or words betrayed a tendency towards such a lapse, she became instantly and palpably most conventional.

Now, in the light of all he had heard from various sources, what could he believe but that she was interested, to say the least, in that other man? Well and miserably he recalled the words of Farquhar, who had served some years at the same station with the Rays: "She's the bonniest little army girl I know, and her head's as level as it is pretty—except on one point. She's her father's daughter and wrapped up in the army. She's always said she'd marry only a soldier. But Maidie's getting wisdom with years, I fancy. Young Foster will be a rich man in spite of himself, for he'll have his mother's fortune, and he's heels over head in love with her."

"But I understood," interposed the general, with a quick glance at Stuyvesant, who had risen as though to get another cigar, "that Ray didn't exactly approve of him."

"Oh, Ray didn't seem to have any special objection to Foster unless it was that he neglected his business to lay siege to her. Foster's a gentleman, has no bad habits, and is the very man nine women out of ten would rejoice in for a husband, and ninety-nine out of ten, if that were a mathematical possibility, would delight in as a son-in-law. He isn't brilliant—buttons would have supplied the lack had he been in the cavalry. I dare say he'll be ass enough to go in for a commission now and sell out his ranch for a song. Then, she'd probably take him."

And then, too, as he strolled thoughtfully up the street, still dimly lighted by the waning moon and dotted at long intervals by tiny electric fires, Stuyvesant went over in mind other little things that had come to his ears, for many men were of a mind with regard to Billy Ray's daughter, and the young officer found himself vaguely weighing the reasons why he should now cease to play the moth,—why he should be winging his flight away from the flame and utterly ignoring the fact that his feet, as though from force of habit, were bearing him steadily towards it. The snap and ring of a bayoneted rifle coming to the charge, the stern voice of a sentry at the crossing of the Calle Faura, brought him to his senses.

"Halt! Who is there?"

"Staff officer, First Division," was the prompt reply, as Stuyvesant looked up in surprise.

"Advance, staff officer, and be recognized," came the response from a tall form in blue, and the even taller white figure stepped forward and stood face to face with the guardian of the night.

"I am Lieutenant Stuyvesant, aide-de-camp to General Vinton," explained the challenged officer, noticing for the first time a little column of dusky men in heavy leathern helmets and belts shuffling away towards the Jesuit College with an old-fashioned diminutive "goose-neck" village engine trailing at their heels.

"Been a fire, sentry?" he asked. "Where was it?"

"Up at Colonel Brent's, sir, I believe. His house fronts the parade-ground. One moment, please! Lieutenant *Who*, sir? The officer of the guard orders us to account for every officer by name." And Stuyvesant, who, in instant alarm, had impulsively started, was again recalled to himself, and, hastily turning back, spoke aloud:

"Stuyvesant my name is. I'll give it at the guard-house as I pass."

Once more he whirled about, his heart throbbing with anxiety. Once more he would have hurried on his way to the Calle San Luis. A fire there! and she, Marion, still so weak!—exhausted, possibly, by the excitement—or distress—or whatever it was that resulted from Brent's sudden presentation of that *carte-de-visite*. He would fly to her at once!

For a third time the sentry spoke, and spoke in no faltering tone. He was an American. He was wearing the rough garb of the private soldier in the ranks of the regulars, but, like scores of other eager young patriots that year, he held the diploma of a great, albeit a foreign, university. He had education, intelligence, and assured social position to back the training and discipline of the soldier. He knew his rights as well as his duties, and that every officer in the service, no matter how high, from commanding general down, was by regulation enjoined to show respect to sentries, and this tall, handsome young swell, with a name that sounded utterly unfamiliar to California ears, was in most unaccountable hurry, and spoke as though he, the sentry, were exceeding his powers in demanding his name. It put Private Thinking Bayonets on his mettle.

"Halt, sir," said he. "My orders are imperative. You'll have to spell that name."

In the nervous anxiety to which Stuyvesant was a prey, the sentry's manner irritated him. It smacked at first of undue, unnecessary authority, yet the soldier in him put the unworthy thought to shame, and, struggling against his impatience, yet most unwillingly, Stuyvesant obediently turned. He had shouldered a musket in a splendid regiment of citizen soldiery whose pride it was that no regular army inspector could pick flaws in their performance of guard and sentry duty. He had brought to the point of his bayonet, time and again, officers far higher in rank than that which he now held. He knew that, whether necessary or not, the sentry's demand was within his rights, and there was no course for him but compliance. He hastened back, and, controlling his voice as much as possible, began:

"You're right, sentry! S-t-u-y"—when through a gate-way across the street north of the Faura came swinging into sight a little squad of armed men.

Again the sentry's challenge, sharp, clear, resonant, rang on the still night air. Three soldiers halted in their tracks, the fourth, with the white chevrons of a corporal on his sleeves, came bounding across the street without waiting for a demand to advance for recognition.

"Same old patrol, Billy," he called, as he neared them. "On the way back to the guard-house." Then, seeing the straps on the officer's shoulders, respectfully saluted. "Couldn't find a trace outside. Keep sharp lookout, Number 6," he added, and turning hurriedly back to his patrol, started with them up the street in the direction Stuyvesant was longing to go.

"Sorry to detain you, sir, and beg pardon for letting him run up on us in that way. We've got extra orders to-night. There's a queer set, mostly natives, in that second house yonder" (and he pointed to a substantial two-story building about thirty paces from the corner). "They got in there while the fire excitement was on. Twice I've seen them peeking out from that door. That's why I dare not leave here and chase after you—after the lieutenant. Now, may I have the name again, sir."

And at last, without interruption, Stuyvesant spelled and pronounced the revered old Dutch patronymic. At last he was able to go unhindered, and now, overcome by anxiety, eagerness, and dread, he hardly knew what, he broke into fleet-footed, rapid run, much to the surprise of the staid patrol which he overtook trudging along on the opposite side of the street, two blocks away, and never halted until again brought up standing by a sentry at the San Luis.

Ten minutes later, while still listening to Brent's oft-repeated tale of the theft, and still quivering a little from excitement, Stuyvesant heard another sound, the rapid, rhythmic beat of dancing footsteps.

"Hullo!" interrupted one of the lingering officers. "Another fire company coming? It's about time more began to arrive, isn't it?"

"It's a patrol—and on the jump, too! What's up, I wonder?" answered Brent, spinning about to face towards the Calle Real. There was an officer with this patrol,—an officer who in his eagerness could barely abide the sentry's challenge.

"Officer of the guard—with patrol," he cried, adding instantly, as he darted into view. "Sentry, which—which way did that officer go? Tall young officer—in white uniform!"

In surprise, the sentry nodded towards the speechless group

standing in front of Brent's, and to them came the boy lieutenant, panting and in manifest excitement. "I beg pardon, colonel," he began, "our sentry, Number 6, was found a minute ago—shot dead—down on the Padre Faura. My men said they saw an officer running from the spot, running this way, and this gentleman—Mr. Stuyvesant, isn't it?"

There was an awed silence, an awkward pause. "I certainly was there not long ago," spoke Stuyvesant, presently. "And Number 6, your sentry, was then all right. I certainly came running—"

"That's all I can hear," was the sharp interruption. "My orders are to arrest you. You're my prisoner, Mr. Stuyvesant," gasped the lad.

"Preposterous!" said Dr. Frank a few minutes later when told by an awe-stricken group what had occurred.

"Preposterous say I!" echoed Brent. "And yet, see here—Oh, of course, you know Major MacNeil, field officer of the day," he added, indicating a tall, thin-faced, gray-mustached officer of regulars who had but just arrived, and who now held forth a gleaming revolver with the words, "I picked this up myself—not ten yards from where he lay."

It was Marion's.

CHAPTER XVI

A solemn assemblage was that at the Ermita quarters of the provost-guard the following day. Officers of rank and soldiers from the ranks, in rusty blue, in gleaming white, in dingy Khaki rubbed shoulders and elbows in the crowded courtyard.

In the presence of death the American remembers that men are born equal, and forgets the ceremonious observance of military courtesies. All voices were lowered, all discussion hushed. There was a spontaneous movement when the division commander entered, and all made way for him without a word, but sturdily stood the rank and file and held their ground against all others, for the preliminary examination, as it might be called, was to take place at ten o'clock.

The dead man was of their own grade, and an ugly story had gone like wildfire through the barracks and quarters that his slayer was a commissioned officer, an aide-de-camp of the general himself, a scion of a distinguished and wealthy family of the greatest city of America, and all official influence, presumably, would be enlisted in his behalf. Therefore, silent, yet determined, were they present in strong force, not in disrespect, not in defiance, but with that calm yet indomitable resolution to see for themselves that justice was done, that soldiers of no other than the Anglo-Saxon race could ever imitate, or that officers, not American, could ever understand, appreciate, and even tacitly approve.

The dead man had died instantly, not in the flush and glory of battle, but in the lonely, yet most honorable, discharge of the sacred duty of the sentinel. Murder most foul was his, and had he been well-nigh a pariah among them,—a man set apart from his kind,—the impulse of his fellow-soldiers would have been to see to it that his death at such a time and on such a duty went not unavenged. As it was, the man who lay there, already stiff and cold, was known among them as one of the bravest, brightest spirits of their whole array, a lad of birth probably more gentle than that of many an officer, of gifts of mind and character superior to those of not a few superiors, a fellow who had won their fellowship as easily as he had learned the duties of the soldier.

A whole battalion in the regulars and dozens of gallant boys in the Idahos and North Dakotas knew Billy Benton and had been full of sympathy when he was picked up one night some three weeks previous, his head laid open by a powerful blow from some blunt instrument, bleeding and senseless. Even when released from hospital a fortnight later he was dazed and queer, was twice reported out of quarters over night and absent from roll-call, but was forgiven because of "previous character," and the belief that he was really not responsible for these soldier solecisms.

One thing seemed to worry him, and that was, as he admitted, that he had been robbed of some papers that he valued. But he soon seemed "all right again," said his fellows, at least to the extent of resuming duty, and when, clean-shaved and in his best attire, he marched on guard that glad October morning, they were betting on him for the first chevrons and speedy commission.

All that his few intimates, the one or two who claimed to know him, could be induced to admit was that his real name was not Benton, and that he had enlisted utterly against the wishes of his kindred. And so, regulars and volunteers alike, they thronged the open *patio* and all approaches thereto, and no officer would now suggest that that court be cleared. It was best that "Thinking Bayonets" should be there to hear and see for himself.

"No, indeed, don't do anything of the kind," said the general promptly when asked half-hesitatingly by the captain of the guard whether he preferred to exclude the men. And in this unusual presence the brief, straightforward examination went on.

First to tell his tale was the corporal of the second relief. He had posted his men between 8.30 and 8.45, Private Benton on Number 6 at the corner of the Calle Real and Padre Faura. That post had been chosen for him as being not very far away from that of the guard, as the young "feller" had not entirely recovered his strength, and the officer of the day had expressed some regret at his having so soon attempted to resume duty, but Benton had laughingly said that he was "all right" and he didn't mean to have other men doing sentry go for him.

"Soon after nine," said the corporal, "I went round warning all the sentries to look out for the tall Filipino and short, squat American, as directed by the officer of the guard. The officer of the guard himself went round about that time personally cautioning the sentries. There was a good deal of fun and excitement just then down the street. Number 9 in the Calle Nueve had shot twice at some fleeing natives who nearly upset him as they dashed round the corner from the Bagumbayan, and he had later mistaken Colonel Brent in his white suit for a Filipino and nervously fired. Numbers 7 and

8 in the side streets mistook the shooting for fire alarm, and Private Benton repeated, in accordance with his orders, but when I (the corporal) saw him he was laughing to kill himself over the Manila fire department."

Benton didn't seem much impressed at first about the thief and the deserter, but towards 9.45, when the corporal again visited his post and the streets were getting quiet, Benton said there were some natives in the second house across the way whose movements puzzled him. They kept coming to the front door and windows and peeping out at him. A patrol came along just then, searching alleyways and yards, and they looked about the premises, while he, Corporal Scott, started west on the Faura to warn Number 4, who was over towards the beach, and while there Major MacNeil, the field officer of the day, came along, and after making inquiries as to what Number 4 had seen and heard and asking him his orders, he turned back to the Faura, Corporal Scott following.

One block west of the Calle Real the major stopped as though to listen to some sound he seemed to have heard in the dark street running parallel with the Real, and then stepped into it as though to examine, so Scott followed, and almost instantly they heard a muffled report "like a pistol inside a blanket," and hastening round into the Faura they found Benton lying on his face in the middle of the street, just at the corner of the Calle Real, stone dead. His rifle they found in the gutter not twenty feet from him.

Scott ran at once to the guard-house three blocks away and gave the alarm. Then the patrol said that a tall officer, running full speed, had passed them, and here the provost-marshal interposed with—

"Never mind what the patrol said. Just tell what you—the

witness—did next."

Scott continued that he and others with the lieutenant, officer of the guard, ran back to Number 6's post, and there stood the major with the pistol.

"When we asked should we search the yards and alleys the major nodded, but the moment he heard the men telling about the running officer he gave the lieutenant orders—"

And again the provost-marshal said "Never mind," the major would describe all that.

And the major did. He corroborated what Corporal Scott had said, and then went on with what happened after Scott was sent to alarm the guard. Barring some opening of shutters and peering out on the part of natives anxious to know the cause of the trouble, there was no further demonstration until Scott and others came running back. But meanwhile something gleaming in the roadway—the Calle Real—about fifteen paces from the corner and up the street—to the north towards the Bagumbayan—and close to the sidewalk attracted his attention.

He stepped thither and picked up—this revolver. By the electric light at the corner he saw that one chamber was empty. When the guard came on the run and he heard of the tall officer fleeing up towards the Bagumbayan, the direction in which the pistol lay, he sent Mr. Wharton—Lieutenant Wharton—with a patrol in pursuit.

The inscription on the pistol revealed its ownership and cast certain suspicions that warranted his action, he believed, in ordering the instant arrest of the officer if found.

Major MacNeil went on to say he "had not yet made the

acquaintance of Lieutenant Stuyvesant, and did not actually know when he gave the order that it *was* Lieutenant Stuyvesant who ran up the street"—and here the major was evidently in a painful position, but faced his duty like a man and told his story without passion or prejudice, despite the fact that he declared the murdered man to be one of the very best young fellows in his battalion, and that he was naturally shocked and angered at his death.

Then the name of Private Reilly was called, and a keen-featured little Irishman stepped forward. It was one of the patrol. Corporal Stamford, first relief, was in charge of it. They had been hunting as far over as the "Knows-a-lady," and on coming back Number 6 told them of some natives at the second house. Corporal Stamford posted him, Reilly, in the first yard near the street to head off any that tried to run out that way, in case they stirred up a mare's nest, and took the other "fellers" and went round by the front. Nothing came of it, but while they were beating up the yards and enclosures Reilly heard Benton challenge, and saw a tall officer come up to be recognized. They had some words,— the officer and the sentry,—he couldn't tell what, but the officer spoke excited like, and all of a sudden jumped away and started as though to run, and Number 6 "hollered" after him, though Reilly didn't clearly understand what was said. "At all events he made him come back, and it—" Here Reilly seemed greatly embarrassed and glanced about the room from face to face in search of help or sympathy. "It seemed to kind of rile the officer. He acted like he wasn't going to come back first off, and then the corporal came along with the patrol and the officer had to wait while Stamford was recognized, and the boys was sayin' Billy had a right to stand the corporal off until the lieutenant said advance him. And we was laughin' about it and sayin' Billy wasn't the boy to make any mistake about his orders, when we heard the lieutenant come a-runnin' swift downt'other side the street and then saw him scootin' it for the open p'rade."

Did the witness recognize the officer?—did he see him plainly?

"Yes, the electric light was burnin' at the corner, and he'd seen him several times driving by the 'barks.'"

Was the officer present?—now?

"Yes," and Reilly's face reddened to meet the hue of his hair.

Reluctantly, awkwardly, pathetically almost, for in no wise did identification, as it happened, depend on his evidence, the little Irish lad turned till his eyes met those of Stuyvesant, sitting pale, calm, and collected by his general's side, and while the eyes of all men followed those of Reilly they saw that, so far from showing resentment or dismay, the young gentleman bowed gravely, reassuringly, as though he would have the witness know his testimony was exactly what it should be and that no blame or reproach attached to him for the telling of what he had seen.

Then Dr. Frank was called, and he gave his brief testimony calmly and clearly. It was mainly about the pistol. He recognized it as one he had seen and examined the previous afternoon at Colonel Brent's quarters on the San Luis. It was lying on a little table in the front veranda. He had closely examined it—could not be mistaken about it, and when he left it was still lying on that table. Who were present when he left? "Other than the immediate family, only Lieutenant Stuyvesant." Had he again visited the colonel's that evening? He had. He returned an hour or so later to dine. The ladies had then left their seats in the veranda, and he noticed that the pistol was no longer on the table; presumed Miss Ray had taken it with her to her room and thought no more about it. As indicated by the inscription, the pistol was her property.

Then Lieutenant Ray was called, but there was no response. In low tone the assistant provost-marshal explained that the orderly sent to Paco with message for Lieutenant Ray returned with the reply that Mr. Ray had two days' leave and was somewhere up-town. He as yet had not been found.

A young officer of artillery volunteered the information that late the previous evening, somewhere about ten, Mr. Ray had called at the Cuartel de Meysic, far over on the north side. He was most anxious to find a soldier named Connelly, who, he said, was at the Presidio at the time the lieutenant's quarters were entered and robbed, and Lieutenant Abercrombie had taken Mr. Ray off in search of the soldier.

Ray not appearing, the examination of Assistant Surgeon Brick began. Brick was the first medical officer to reach the scene of the murder. Benton was then stone dead, and brief examination showed the hole of a bullet of large calibre— probably pistol, 44—right over the heart. The coarse blue uniform shirt and the fine undergarment of Lisle thread showed by burn and powder-stain that the pistol had been close to or even against the breast of the deceased. The bullet was lodged, he believed, under the shoulder-blade, but no post-mortem had yet been permitted, a circumstance the doctor referred to regretfully, and it was merely his opinion, based on purely superficial examination, that death was instantaneous, the result of the gunshot wound referred to. Dr. Brick further gave it as his professional opinion that post-mortem should be no longer delayed.

And then at last came Stuyvesant's turn to speak for himself, and in dead silence all men present faced him and listened with bated breath to his brief, sorrowful words.

He was the officer halted by the sentry on Number 6 and called upon to come back. The sentry did not catch his name and had to have it spelled. He frankly admitted his impatience, but denied all anger at the enforced detention. The information about the fire at Colonel Brent's had caused him anxiety and alarm, and as soon as released by the sentry he had run, had passed the patrol on the run, but there had been no altercation, no misunderstanding even. The sentry had carried out his orders in a soldierly way that compelled the admiration of the witness, and before leaving him Stuyvesant had told him that he had done exactly right. The news that the sentry was found dead five minutes thereafter was a shock. Lieutenant Stuyvesant declared he carried no fire-arms whatever that night and was utterly innocent of the sentry's death. He recognized, he said, the revolver exhibited by Major MacNeil. He did not hesitate to admit that he had seen and examined it late the previous afternoon at the quarters of Colonel Brent, that he had actually put it in his trousers pocket not two minutes before he left the house to go in search of Lieutenant Ray, but he solemnly declared that as he left the veranda he placed the pistol on a little table just to the right of the broad entrance to the salon, within that apartment, and never saw it again until it was produced here.

Frank, candid, "open and aboveboard" as was the manner of the witness, it did not fail to banish in great measure the feeling of antagonism that had first existed against him in the crowded throng. But in the cold logic of the law and the chain of circumstantial evidence they plainly saw that every statement, even that of Stuyvesant himself, bore heavily against him. A lawyer, had he been represented by counsel, would have permitted no such admissions as he had made. A gentleman, unschooled in the law, preferred the frank admission to the distress of seeing Mrs. Brent—and perhaps others—called into that presence to testify to his having had the pistol with him when he left the gallery.

Brent in his bewilderment had blurted out his wife's words in the hearing of the provost-marshal's people late the night before, and he and his household were yet to be called, and when called would have to say that though they passed and possibly repassed through the salon between the moment of Stuyvesant's departure and that of their going out to dinner, not one of their number noticed even so bright and gleaming an object as Maidie's revolver. True, the lights were not brilliant in the salon. True, the little table stood back against the wall five or six feet from the door-way. Still, that pistol was a prominent object, and a man must have been in extraordinary haste indeed to leave a loaded weapon "lying round loose" in the hall.

That was the way "Thinking Bayonets" argued it, and soldiers by the score crowding the sidewalk and entrance and unable to force their way in, or even to make room for a most importunate female struggling on the outskirts, hung on the words of an orderly who, despatched in further search of Lieutenant Ray, was forcing a way out.

"How is it going?" said he. "Why, that young feller's just as good as hanging himself. He admits having had the pistol that did the business."

Ten minutes later a Filipino servant went to answer an imperative rap at the panel in the massive door of No. 199 Calle San Luis. Dr. Frank had been early to see his patient, and had enjoined upon Mrs. Brent and Miss Porter silence as to last night's tragedy. Not until she was stronger was Miss Ray to be allowed to know of the murder of Private Benton. "By that time," said he, "we shall be able to clear up this— mystery—I *hope*."

The colonel had gone round to the police-station. Mrs. Brent, nervous and unhappy, had just slipped out for ten seconds, as she said to Miss Porter, to see an old army chum and friend who lived only three doors away. Miss Porter, who had been awake hours of the night, had finally succeeded, as she believed, in reading Maidie to sleep, and then, stretching herself upon the bamboo couch across the room, was, the next thing she knew, aroused by voices.

Sandy Ray had entered so noiselessly that she had not heard, but Maidie had evidently been expecting him. In low, earnest tone he was telling the result of his search the night before. She heard the words:

"Connelly is down with some kind of fever in hospital and hasn't seen or heard anything of any one even faintly resembling Foster. Then I found your old friend the brakeman. General Vinton has got him a good place in the quartermaster's department, and he tells me he knows nothing, has seen and heard nothing. Now I'm going to division headquarters to find Stuyvesant."

"And then," said Miss Porter, "my heart popped up into my throat and I sprang from the sofa." But too late. An awful, rasping voice at the door-way stilled the soft Kentucky tones and filled the room with dread.

"Then you've no time to lose, young man. It's high time somebody besides me set out to help him. That other young man you call Foster lies dead at the police-station,—killed by *your* pistol, Miss Ray, and Mr. Stuyvesant goes to jail for it."

CHAPTER XVII

In so far as human foresight could provide against the cabling to the States of tremendous tales that had little or no foundation, the commanding general had been most vigilant. The censorship established over the despatches of the correspondents had nipped many a sensation in the bud and insured to thousands of interested readers at home far more truthful reports of the situation at Manila than would have been the case had the press been given full swing.

Yet with Hong-Kong only sixty hours away, there was nothing to prevent their writing to and wiring from that cosmopolitan port, and here, at least, was a story that would set the States ablaze before it could be contradicted, and away it went, fast as the Esmeralda could speed it across the China Sea and the wires, with it, well-nigh girdle the globe.

A gallant young volunteer, Walter Foster of Ohio, serving in the regulars under the assumed name of Benton, foully murdered by Lieutenant Gerard Stuyvesant of New York! A love affair at the bottom of it all! Rivals for the hand of a fair army girl, daughter of a distinguished officer of the regular service! Lieutenant Stuyvesant under guard! Terrible wrath of the soldier's comrades! Lynching threatened! Speedy justice demanded! The maiden prostrated! Identification of the victim by Miss Zenobia Perkins, Vice-President and

Accredited Representative for the Philippine Islands of the Society of Patriotic Daughters of America! Army circles in Manila stirred to the bottom! etc., etc.

Joyous reading this for friends and kindred in the far-distant States! Admirable exhibit of journalistic enterprise! The Hong Kong papers coming over in course of another week were full of it, and of appropriate comment on the remarkable depravity of the American race, and Chicago journals, notably the *Palladium*, bristled with editorial explosions over the oft-repeated acts of outrage and brutality on part of the American officer to the friendless private in the American ranks.

And thousands of honest, well-meaning men and women, who had seen, year after year, lie after lie, one stupendous story after another, punctured, riddled, and proved a vicious and malignant slander, swallowed this latest one whole, and marvelled that the American officer could be the monster the paper proved him to be.

But one woman at last and at least was happy, perched now on a pinnacle of fame, and in the Patriotic Daughters of America as represented by their Vice-President and Accredited Representative in the Philippines, virtue and rectitude reigned triumphant. Zenobia Perkins was in her glory. Of all the citizens or soldiers of the United States in and about Manila, male or female, staff or supply, signal or hospital corps, Red Cross or crossed cannon, rifles, or sabres, this indomitable woman was now the most sought after—the most in demand. Her identification of the dead man had been positive and complete.

"I suspected instantly," she declared in presence of the assembled throng, "when I heard Lieutenant Stuyvesant had shot a soldier, just who it might be. I remembered the young man who disappeared from the train before we got to Oakland. I suspected him the moment the corporal told me about the mysterious young man trying to see Miss Ray. I had my carriage chase right after him to the Nozaleda and caught him, half-running, half-staggering, and I took him driving until he got ca-amed down and told him he needn't worry any more. He was among friends at last, and the P. D. A.'s would take care of him and guard his secret and see him done right by. Oh, yes, I did! We weren't going to see an innocent boy shot as a deserter when he didn't know what he was doing. He wouldn't admit at first that he was Walter Foster at all, but at last, when he saw I was sure it was him, he just broke right down and as much as owned right up. He said he'd been slugged or sand-bagged three weeks before and robbed of money and of papers of value that he needed to help him in his trouble. He asked me what steps could be taken to help a poor fellow accused of desertion. He didn't dare say anything to any of the officers' 'cause the men he trusted at all—one or two well-educated young fellows like himself—found out that he'd be shot if found guilty. The only thing he could do was make a good record for himself in the infantry, and having done that he could later on hope for mercy. He asked a heap of questions, and I just told him to keep a stiff upper lip and we'd see him through, and he plucked up courage and said he believed he'd be able to have hope again;—at all events he'd go on duty right off. When I asked him how he dared go to Colonel Brent's, where at any time Lieutenant Ray might recognize him, he said he never *did* except when he knew Lieutenant Ray was out of the way. Then I tried to get him to tell what he expected to gain by seeing Miss Ray, and he was confused and said he was so upset all over he really didn't know that he had been there so often. He thought if he could see her and tell her the whole story she could have influence enough to get him out of his scrape. He was going to tell me the whole story, but patrols and sentries were getting too thick, and he had to get somewhere to change his dress for roll-call, and I gave him my address and he was to come and see me in two days, and now he's killed, and it ain't for me to say why—or who did it."

Benton's murder was certainly the sensation of the week in Manila, for there were features connected with the case that made it still more perplexing, even mysterious.

Major Farquhar, who must have seen young Foster frequently at Fort Averill, had been sent to survey the harbor of Iloilo and could not be reached in time, but Dr. Frank, called in course of the day to identify the remains, long and carefully studied the calm, waxen features of the dead soldier, and said with earnest conviction:

"This is undoubtedly the young man who appeared at Colonel Brent's and whom I sought to question, but who seemed to take alarm at once and, with some confused apology, backed away. He was dressed very neatly in the best white drilling sack-coat and trousers as made in Manila, with a fine straw hat and white shoes and gloves, but he had a fuzzy beard all over his face then, and his manner was nervous and excitable. His eyes alone showed that he was unstrung, bodily and mentally. I set him down for a crank or some one just picking up from serious illness. The city is full of new-comers, and as yet no one knows how many strangers have recently come to town. I saw him only that once in a dim light, but am positive in this identification."

Two or three non-commissioned officers of Benton's regiment were examined. Their stories were concise and to the point. The young soldier had come with the recruits from San Francisco along late in August. He was quiet, well-mannered, attended strictly to his own business, and was eager to learn everything about his duties. They "sized him up" as a young man of education and good family who hadn't influence enough to get a commission and so had enlisted to win it. He had money, but no bad habits. He helped in the office with the regimental papers, and could have been excused from all duty and made clerk, but wouldn't be. He said he'd help whenever they wanted him, but he didn't wish to be excused from guard or drills or patrol or picket—said he wanted to learn all there was in it. Even the rough fellows in the ranks couldn't help liking him. He had a pleasant word for everybody that didn't bother him with questions. He made one or two acquaintances, but kept mostly to himself; never got any letters from America, but there were two from Hong Kong, perhaps more. If he wrote letters himself, he posted them in town. They never went with the company mail from the *cuartel*. Everybody seemed to know that Benton wasn't his own name, but that was nothing. The main thing queer about him was that he got a pass whenever he could and went by himself, most generally out to Paco, where the cavalry were, yet he said he didn't know anybody there. It was out Paco way on the Calzada Herran, close to the corner of the Singalon road, the patrol picked him up with his head laid open, and he'd been flighty pretty much ever since and troubled about being robbed. Seemed all right again, however, when reporting for duty, and perfectly sane and straight then.

Two very bright young soldiers, Clark and Hunter, were called in for their statements. They, too, had enlisted in a spirit of patriotism and desire for adventure; never knew Benton till the voyage was nearly over, then they seemed to drift together, as it were, and kept up their friendship after reaching Manila. Benton was not his real name, and he was not a graduate of any American college. He had been educated abroad and spoke French and German. No, they did not know what university he attended. He was frank and pleasant so long as nobody tried to probe into his past; never heard him mention Lieutenant Stuyvesant. All three of them,

Benton, Clarke, and Hunter, had observed that young officer during the month as he drove by barracks, sometimes with the general, sometimes alone, but they did not know his name, and nothing indicated that Benton had any feeling against him or that he had seen him. They admitted having conveyed the idea to comrades that they knew more about Benton than they would tell, but it was a "bluff." Everybody was full of speculation and curiosity, and—well, just for the fun of the thing, they "let on," as they said, that they were in his confidence, but they weren't, leastwise to any extent. They knew he had money, knew he went off by himself, and warned him to keep a look out or he'd be held up and robbed some night.

The only thing of any importance they had to tell was that one day, just before his misfortune, Benton was on guard and posted as sentry over the big Krupps in the Spanish battery at the west end of the Calle San Luis. Clarke and Hunter had a kodak between them and a consuming desire to photograph those guns. The sentries previously posted there refused to let them come upon the parapet,—said it was "'gainst orders." Benton said that unless positive orders were given to him to that effect, he would not interfere. So they got a pass on the same day and Benton easily got that post,—men didn't usually want it, it was such a bother,—but, unluckily, with the post Benton got the very orders they dreaded. So when they would have made the attempt he had to say, "No." They came away crestfallen, and stumbled on two sailor-looking men who, from the shelter of a heavy stone revetment wall, were peering with odd excitement of manner at Benton, who was again marching up and down his narrow post, a very soldierly figure.

"That young feller drove you back, did he?" inquired one of them, a burly, thick-set, hulking man of middle height. "Puttin' on considerable airs, ain't he? What's he belong to?"

"—th Infantry," answered Clarke shortly, not liking the stranger's looks, words, or manner, and then pushed on; but the stranger followed, out of sight of the sentry now, and wanted to continue the conversation.

"Sure he ain't in the cavalry?" asked the same man.

"Cocksure!" was the blunt reply. "What's it to you, anyhow?"

"Oh, nothin'; thought I'd seen him before. Know his name?"

"Name's Benton, far as I know. Come on, Hunter," said Clarke, obviously unwilling to stay longer in such society, and little more was thought of it for the time being; but now the provost-marshal's assistant wished further particulars. Was there anything unusual about the questioner's teeth? And a hundred men looked up in surprise and suddenly rearoused interest.

"Yes, sir," said Clarke, "one tooth was missing, upper jaw, next the big eye-tooth;" and as the witness stood down the general and the questioning officer beamed on each other and smiled.

An adjournment was necessitated during the early afternoon. Lieutenant Ray's statement was desired, also that of Private Connelly of the artillery, and an effort had been made through the officers of the cavalry at Paco to find some of the recruits who were of the detachment now quite frequently referred to in that command as "the singed cats." But it transpired that most of them had been assigned to troops of their regiment not yet sent to Manila, only half the regiment being on duty—foot duty at that—in the Philippines. The only man among them who had travelled with Foster from Denver as far as Sacramento was the young recruit, Mellen. He was on outpost, but would be relieved and sent to Ermita as quickly as possible.

Connelly, said the surgeon at the Cuartel de Meysic, was too ill to be sent thither, unless on a matter of vital importance, and Sandy Ray, hastening from Maidie's bedside in response to a summons, was met by the tidings that a recess had been ordered, and that he would be sent for again when needed.

Everywhere in Malate, Ermita, Paco, and, for that matter, the barracks and quarters of Manila, the astonishing story was the topic of all tongues that day. Among the regulars by this time the tale of Foster's devotion to Maidie Ray was well known, while that of Stuyvesant's later but assiduous courtship was rapidly spreading.

Men spoke in murmurs and with sombre faces, and strove to talk lightly on other themes, but the tragedy, with all the honored names it involved, weighed heavily upon them. Stuyvesant came to them, to be sure, a total stranger, but Vinton had long known him, and that was enough. His name, his lineage, his high position socially, all united to throw discredit on the grave suspicion that attached to him. Yet, here they were, brought face to face, rivals for the hand of as lovely a girl as the army ever knew. It was even possible that Foster was the aggressor. Reilly's reluctant words gave proof that discussion of some kind had occurred, and Stuyvesant broke away and was apparently wrathful at being compelled to go back; then more words, longer detention; then a swift-running form, Stuyvesant's, away from the scene; then the fatal pistol; and against this chain of circumstances only the unsupported statement of the accused that he left that revolver on the table in the salon, left it where it was never afterwards seen. No wonder men shook their heads.

It was three in the afternoon when the examination was resumed. Meantime, from all over Manila came the correspondents, burning with zeal and impatience, for the Esmeralda was scheduled to leave at five, and a stony-hearted censor at the Ayuntamiento had turned down whole pages of thrilling "copy" that would cost three dollars a word to send to the States, but sell for thirty times as much when it got there.

"Despite the positive identification of the remains," wrote one inspired journalist, "by such an unimpeachable and intelligent woman as Zenobia Perkins, who attended the murdered lad after he was so severely burned upon the train,—despite the equally positive recognition by that eminent and distinguished surgeon, Dr. Frank, this military satrap and censor dares to say that not until the identity of the deceased is established to the satisfaction of the military authorities will the report be cabled. How long will the people of America submit to such tyrannical dictation?"

When the provost-marshal himself, with his assistants and Vinton and Stuyvesant, returned at three and found Zenobia the vortex of a storm of questioners, the centre of a circle of rapid-writing scribes, these latter could have sworn—did swear, some of them—that, far from expediting matters in order that a full report might be sent by the Esmeralda, the officials showed a provoking and exasperating disposition to prolong and delay them.

And even at this time and at this distance, with all his regard, personal and professional, for the official referred to, the present chronicler is unable entirely to refute the allegation.

Out in the street a score of carriages and as many *quilez* and *carromattas* stood waiting by the curb, and gallant Captain Taylor, of the Esmeralda, could have added gold by the hundred to his well-earned store would he but have promised to hold his ship until the court—not the tide—served. But an aide of the commanding general had driven to the ship towards two o'clock and said something to that able seaman,—no power of the press could tell what,—and all importunity as to delaying his departure there was but one reply,—

"Five sharp, and not a second later!"

It was after three—yes, long after—that witnesses of consequence came up for examination. Dr. Brick had got the floor and was pleading *post-mortem* at once. In this climate and under such conditions decomposition would be so rapid, said he, that "by tomorrow his own mother couldn't recognize him." But the provost-marshal drawled that he didn't see that further mutilation would promote the possibility of recognition, and Brick was set aside.

It was quarter to four when young Mellen was bidden to tell whether he knew, and what he knew of, the deceased, and all men hushed their very breath as the lad was conducted to the blanket-shrouded form under the overhanging gallery in the open *patio*. The hospital steward slowly turned down the coverlet, and Mellen, well-nigh as pallid as the corpse, was bidden to look. Look he did, long and earnestly. The little weights that some one had placed on the eyelids were lifted; the soft hair had been neatly brushed; the lips were gently closed; the delicate, clear-cut features wore an expression of infinite peace and rest; and Mellen slowly turned and, facing the official group at the neighboring table, nodded.

"You think you recognize the deceased?" came the question. "If so, what was his name?"

"I think so, yes, sir. It's Foster—at least that's what I heard it was."

"Had you ever known him?—to speak to?"

"He was in the same detachment on the train. Don't know as I ever spoke to him, sir," was the answer.

"But you think you know him by sight? Where did you first notice him?"

"Think it was Ogden, sir. I didn't pay much attention before that. A man called Murray knew him and got some money from him. That's how I came to notice him. The rest of us hadn't any to speak of."

"Ever see him again to speak to or notice particularly after you left Ogden? Did he sit near you?" was the somewhat caustic query.

"No, sir, only just that once."

"But you are sure this is the man you saw at Ogden?"

Mellen turned uneasily, unhappily, and looked again into the still and placid face. That meeting was on a glaring day in June. This was a clouded afternoon in late October and nearly five months had slipped away. Yet he had heard the solemn story of murder and had never, up to now, imagined there could be a doubt. In mute patience the sleeping face seemed appealing to him to speak for it, to own it, to stand between it and the possibility of its being buried friendless, unrecognized.

"It's—it's him or his twin brother, sir," said Mellen.

"One question more. Had you heard before you came here who was killed?"

"Yes, sir. They said it was Foster."

And now, with pencils swiftly plying, several young civilians were edging to the door.

James Farnham was called, and a sturdy young man, with keen, weather-beaten face, stepped into the little open space before the table. Three fingers were gone from the hand he instinctively held up, as though expecting to be sworn. His testimony was decidedly a disappointment. Farnham said that he was brakeman of that train and would know some of that squad of recruits anywhere, but this one,—well, he remembered talking to one man at Ogden, a tall, fine-looking young feller something very like this one. This might have been him or it might not. He couldn't even be sure that this was one of the party. He really didn't know. But there was a chap called Murray that he'd remember easy enough anywhere.

And then it was after four and the race for the Esmeralda began. It was utterly unnecessary, said certain bystanders, to question any more members of the guard, but the provost-marshal did, and not until 4.30 did he deign to send for the most important witness of all, the brother of the young girl to whom the deceased had been so devotedly attached. They had not long to wait, for Sandy Ray happened to be almost at the door.

The throng seemed to take another long breath, and then to hold it as, the few preliminaries answered, Mr. Ray was bidden to look at the face of the deceased. Pale, composed, yet with infinite sadness of mien, the young officer, campaign hat in hand, stepped over to the trestle, and the steward again slowly withdrew the light covering, again exposing that placid face.

The afternoon sunshine was waning. The bright glare of the mid-day hours had given place within the enclosure to the softer, almost shadowy light of early eve. Ray had but just come in from the street without where the slanting sunbeams bursting through the clouds beat hot upon the dazzling walls, and his eyes had not yet become accustomed to the change. Reverently, pityingly, he bent and looked upon the features of the dead. An expression, first of incredulity, then of surprise, shot over his face.

He closed his eyes a second as though to give them strength for sterner test, and then, bending lower, once more looked; carefully studied the forehead, eyebrows, lashes, mouth, nose, and hair, then, straightening up, he slowly faced the waiting room and said,—

"I never set eyes on this man in my life before to-day."

CHAPTER XVIII

To say that Mr. Ray's abrupt announcement was a surprise to the dense throng of listeners is putting it mildly. To say that it was received with incredulity on part of the soldiery, and concern, if not keen apprehension, by old friends of Sandy's father who were present, is but a faint description of the effect of the lad's emphatic statement.

To nine out of ten among the assembly the young officer was a total stranger. To more than nine out of ten the identification of the dead as Walter Foster, Maidie Ray's luckless lover, was already complete, and many men who have made up their minds are incensed at those who dare to differ from them.

True, Mr. Stuyvesant had said that the sentry, Number 6, did not remind him except in stature, form, and possibly in features, of the recruit he knew as Foster on the train. He did not speak like him. But, when closely questioned by the legal adviser of the provost-marshal's department—the officer who conducted most of the examination with much of the manner of a prosecuting attorney, Mr. Stuyvesant admitted that he had only seen Foster once to speak to, and that was at night in the dim light of the Sacramento station on what might be called the off-side of the train, where the shadows were heavy, and while the face of the young soldier was partially covered with a bandage. Yet Vinton attached importance to his aide-de-camp's opinion, and when Ray came out flat-footed, as it were, in support of Stuyvesant's views, the general was visibly gratified.

But, except for these very few, Ray had spoken to unbelieving ears. Sternly the military lawyer took him in hand and began to probe. No need to enter into details. In ten minutes the indignant young gentleman, who never in his life had told a lie, found himself the target of ten score of hostile eyes, some wrathful, some scornful, some contemptuous, some insolent, some only derisive, but all, save those of a few silently observant officers, threatening or at least inimical.

Claiming first that he knew Walter Foster well (and, indeed, it seemed to him he did, for his mother's letters to the Big Horn ranch had much to say of Maidie's civilian admirer, though Maidie herself could rarely be induced to speak of him), Ray was forced to admit that he had met him only twice or thrice during a brief and hurried visit to Fort Averill to see his loved ones before they moved to Fort Leavenworth, and then he owned he paid but little attention to the sighing swain. Questioned as to his opportunities of studying and observing Foster, Sandy had been constrained to say that he hadn't observed him closely at all. He "didn't want to—exactly." They first met, it seems, in saddle. The winter weather was glorious at Averill. They had a fine pack of hounds; coursing for jack-rabbit was their favorite sport, and, despite the fact that Foster had a beautiful and speedy horse, "his seat was so poor and his hand so jerky he never managed to get up to the front," said Sandy.

It was not brought out in evidence, but the fact was that Sandy could never be got to look on Foster with the faintest favor as a suitor for his sister's hand. A fellow who could neither ride, shoot, nor spar—whose accomplishments were solely of the carpet and perhaps the tennis-court—the boy had no use for. He and Maidie rode as though born to the saddle. He had seen Foster in an English riding-suit and English saddle and an attempt at the English seat, but decidedly without the deft English hand on his fretting hunter's mouth the one day that they appeared in field together, and the sight was too much for Sandy. That night at dinner, and the later dance, Foster's perfection of dress and manner only partially redeemed him in Sandy's eyes, and—well—really, that was about all he ever had seen of Foster.

Questioned as to his recollection of Foster's features, stature, etc., Sandy did his best, and only succeeded in portraying the deceased almost to the life. Except, he said, Foster had long, thick, curving eyelashes, and "this man hasn't"—but it was remembered that brows and lashes both were singed off in the fire. So that point failed. Questioned as to whether he realized that his description tallied closely with the appearance of the deceased, Sandy said that that all might be, but still "this isn't Foster." Questioned as to whether, if the deceased were again to have the color and action,—the life that Foster had a year ago,—might not the resemblance to Foster be complete?—Sandy simply "couldn't tell."

Nearly an hour was consumed in trying to convince him he must, or at least might, be mistaken, but to no purpose. He mentioned a card photograph of Foster in ranch costume that would convince the gentlemen, he thought, that there was no such very strong resemblance, and a note was written to Miss Porter asking her to find and send the picture in question. It came, a cabinet photo of a tall, slender, well-built young fellow with dark eyes and brows and thick, curving lashes and oval, attractive face, despite its boyishness, and nine men out of ten who saw and compared it with the face of the dead declared it looked as though it had been taken for the latter perhaps a year or so agone. Ray had hurt his own case, and, when excused to return to his sister's side, went forth into the gathering twilight stricken with the consciousness that he was believed to have lied in hopes of averting scandal from that sister's name.

And on the morrow with that *post-mortem*, so insisted on by Brick, no longer delayed, the dead again lay mutely awaiting the final action of the civil-military authorities, and to the surprise of the officers and guards, before going to the daily routine that kept him from early morn till late at night in his beleaguered office, Drayton came and bowed his gray head and gazed with sombre eyes into the sleeping features now before him.

A pinched and tired look was coming over the waxen face that had been so calm and placid, as though in utter weariness over this senseless delay. Drayton had been told of young Ray's almost astounding declaration, and officers of the law half expected him to make some adverse comment thereon, but he did not. Alert correspondents, amazed to see the corps commander at such a place and so far from the Ayuntamiento, surrounded him as he would have retaken his seat in his carriage, and clamored for something as coming from him in the way of an expression of opinion, which, with grave courtesy, the general declined to give, but could not prevent appearing a week later in a thousand papers and in a dozen different forms—ferried over to Hong Kong by the Shogun or some other ship, and cabled thence to waiting Christendom.

Drayton had his own reasons for wishing to see the remains, then Vinton, and later Ray, and as his movements were closely followed, the wits of the correspondents were sorely taxed. But the examination was to be resumed at nine. A rumor was running wild that Miss Ray herself was to be summoned to appear, and Drayton had to be dropped in favor of a more promising sensation.

It began with dreary surgical technicalities. The heavy bullet had traversed the ascending aorta "near its bifurcation," said Brick, who, though only an autopsical adjunct, was permitted to speak for his associates. Death, said he, had resulted from shock and was probably instantaneous. No other cause could be attributed. No other wound was discovered. No marks of scuffle except "some unimportant scratches" on the shoulder. The bullet was found to weigh exactly the same as those of the unexploded cartridges in poor Maidie's prized revolver, and though Brick would gladly have kept the floor and told very much more, the provost-marshal as gladly got rid of him, for, despite the unwillingness of the medical officers at the Cuartel de Meysic, Connelly had been trundled down to Ermita in a springy ambulance and was presently awaiting his turn.

The moment his coming was announced, Connelly was ushered in and Brick shut off short.

A nurse and doctor were with the sturdy little Irishman, and he needed but brief instruction as to what was wanted. Taken to the trestle and bidden to look upon the face of the deceased and say, if he could, who it was, Connelly looked long and earnestly, and then turned feebly but calmly to the attentive array.

"If it wasn't that this looks much thinner," said he, "I'd say it was a man who 'listed with our detachment at Denver last June, about the first week. The name was Foster. He disappeared somewhere between Sacramento and Oakland, and I never saw him again."

Questioned as to whether there was any mark by which the

recruit could be known, Connelly said that he was present when Foster was physically examined, and he never saw a man with a whiter skin; there wasn't a mark on him anywhere then that he could remember. Bidden to tell what he knew of Foster, the young artilleryman was given a seat, and somewhat feebly proceeded. Foster was bound to enlist, he said, was of legal age and looked it; gave his full name, his home and business; said he owned a ranch down in New Mexico near Fort Averill; didn't know enough to go in for a commission and was determined to enlist and serve as a private soldier in the cavalry. He had good clothes and things that he put in a trunk and expressed back to Averill, keeping only a valise full of underwear, etc., but that was burned up on the car afterwards. Two days later, before they started for the West, a man who said his name was Murray came to the rendezvous and asked for Foster, who was then being drilled. A detachment was to start the next day, and anybody could see that Foster wasn't glad to welcome Murray by any means, but on that very evening Murray said that he too wished to enlist and go with his "friend." He squeezed through the physical examination somehow, and they took him along, though nobody liked his looks.

Then Connelly told what he could of the fire and of Foster's subsequent disappearance, also of Murray and Murray's misconduct. They asked Connelly about Lieutenant Stuyvesant, and here Connelly waxed almost eloquent, certainly enthusiastic, in Stuyvesant's praise. Somebody went so far, however, as to ask whether he had ever seen any manifestation of ill-will between Stuyvesant and Recruit Foster, whereat Connelly looked astonished, seemed to forget his fever, and to show something akin to indignation.

"No, indeed!" said he. There was nothing but good-will of the heartiest kind everywhere throughout the detachment except for that one blackguard, Murray. They all felt most grateful to the lieutenant, and so far as he knew they'd all do most anything for him, all except Murray, but he was a tough, he was a biter, and here the sick man feebly uplifted his hand and pointed to the bluish-purple marks at the base of the thumb.

"Murray did that," said Connelly simply. "He was more like a beast than a man."

But the examiners did not seem interested in Murray. General Vinton, who had again entered and was a close listener, and was observed to be studying the witness closely, presently beckoned to one of the doctors and said a word in undertone to him. The medico shook his head. There was a lull in the proceedings a moment. Connelly was too sick a man to be kept there long, and his doctor plainly showed his anxiety to get him away. The crowd too wanted him to go. He had told nothing especially new except that Murray and Foster were acquainted, and Murray enlisted because Foster had.

"Everybody" said by this time this must be Foster's body. What "everybody" wanted was to get Connelly out of the way now, then perhaps—*another* fever patient might be summoned, for they couldn't expect to keep those remains another day. There was widespread, if unspoken, hope among the score of correspondents that the provost-marshal would feel that he must summon Miss Ray.

But before the examiners could decide there came an unexpected scene. Vinton went over, bent, and whispered to the provost-marshal, who looked up, nodded, and glanced towards the witness, sitting flushed and heavy-eyed, but patient, across the room. Vinton was plainly asking something, and to the manifest displeasure of many of the crowd the little Irishman was again accosted.

"You say Murray was a biter and bit you so that the marks last to this day. Did you take note of any peculiarity in his teeth?"

"Yes, sir. One of 'em was gone near the front, right-hand side, next to the big yellow eye-tooth."

"Would that make a peculiar mark on human flesh?"

"Yes, sir," answered Connelly, holding up his hand again and showing the scar, now nearly five months old.

"Steward," said the officer placidly, "uncover the shoulder there and let Connelly look at the mark Dr. Brick referred to."

Connelly did. He studied the purplish discolorations in the milky skin, and excitement, not altogether febrile, suddenly became manifest in his hot, flushed face. Then he held forth one hand, palm uppermost, eagerly compared the ugly scars at the base of the thumb with the faint marks on the broad, smooth shoulder, and turned back to the darkened room. With hand uplifted he cried:

"Major,"—and now he was trembling with mingled weakness and eagerness,—"I knew that man Murray was following this young feller to squeeze money out of him, and when he couldn't get it by threats, he tried by force. He's followed him clear to Manila, and that's his mark sure's this is!—sure's there's a God in heaven!"

CHAPTER XIX

There came a time of something more than anxiety and worry for all who knew Gerard Stuyvesant,—for those who loved Marion Ray,—and Sandy was a sorrow-laden man. Vinton could not stand between his favorite aide-de-camp and the accusation laid at his door. Frank and his most gifted fellow-surgeons were powerless to prevent the relapse that came to Marion and bore her so close to the portals of the great beyond that there were days and nights when the blithe spirit seemed flitting away from its fragile tenement, and November was half gone before the crisis was so far past that recovery could be pronounced only a question of time. Oh, the strain of those long, long, sleepless days of watching, waiting, hoping, praying, yet days wherein the watchers could nurse and help and *act*. Oh, the blackness, the misery of the nights of watching, waiting in helplessness, well-nigh in despair, for the coming of the next "cable!" the consciousness of utter impotence to help or to do! the realization that a priceless life is ebbing away, while they who gave it—they to whom it is so infinitely precious—are at the very opposite ends of the earth! Oh, the tremulous opening of those fateful messages, the breathless reading of the cipher, the awful suspense of the search through Cable Code pages that dance and swim before the straining eyes! Oh, the meek acceptance of still further suspense! the almost piteous thankfulness that all is not yet lost, that hope is not

Charles King

yet abandoned! Strong men break down and add years to those they have lived. Gentle women sway and totter at last until relief comes to them through God-given tears.

In a fever-stricken camp in Southern swamplands a father waked night after night, walking the hospitals where his brave lads lay moaning, seeing in their burning misery, hearing in their last sigh, the sufferings of a beloved child. By the bedside of her youngest, her baby boy as she would ever call the lad, who lay there in delirium, knelt a mother who, as she nursed and soothed this one, prayed without ceasing for that other, that beloved daughter for whom the Death Angel crouched and waited under the tropic skies of the far Philippines. Ah, there were suffering and distress attendant on that strange, eventful epoch in the nation's history that even the press said nothing about, and that those who knew it speak of only in deep solemnity and awe to-day. It was mid-November before they dared to hope. It was December when once again Maid Marion was lifted to her lounging-chair overlooking the Bagumbayan, and little by little began picking up once more the threads that were so nearly severed for all time, and as health and strength slowly returned, hearing the tidings of the busy, bustling world about her.

Others too had known anxiety as sore as that which had so lined the face of Colonel Ray and trebled the silver in the soft hair of Marion, his wife. Well-nigh distracted, a mother sped across the continent to the Pacific, there to await the coming of her son's remains.

From the night of Walter Foster's disappearance at Carquinez no word of his existence came to give her hope, no trace of his movements until, late in August, there was brought to her the cabled message:

"Alive, well, but in trouble. Have written."

And this was headed Yokohama. Not until October did that longed-for, prayed-for letter come,—a selfish letter, since it gave no really adequate excuse for the long weeks of silence, and only told that the boy had been in hiding, almost in terror of his life. While still dazed by the shock of the fire and smarting from his burns, wrote Walter, he had wandered from the cars at Port Costa. He had encountered "most uncongenial persons," he said, among the recruits, and never realizing that it was desertion, war-time desertion at that, had determined to get back to Sacramento and join some other command. Yes. There was another reason, but—one "mother couldn't appreciate." Unknown to all but one of his comrades on the train, he had abundant money, realized from the sale of horses and cattle at the ranch. It was in a buckskin belt about his waist, and this money bought him "friends" who took him by water to Sacramento, found him secret lodgings, procured suitable clothing, and later spirited him off to San Francisco.

But these money-bought friends showed the cloven hoof, threatened to give him over to the military authorities to be tried for his life unless he would pay a heavy sum. They had him virtually a prisoner. He could only stir abroad at night, and then in company with his jailers.

There was a man, he wrote, who had a grudge against him, a man discharged from the ranch, who followed him to Denver and enlisted in the same party, a man he was most anxious to get rid of, and the first thing he knew that fellow, who, he supposed, had gone on to Manila, turned up in disguise and joined forces with his tormentors. That drove him to desperation, nerved him to one sublime effort, and one night he broke away and ran. He was fleet of foot, they were heavy with drink, and he dodged them among the wharves and piers, took refuge on a coast steamer, and found himself two days later at Portland.

Here he bethought him of an old friend, and succeeded in finding a man he well knew he could trust, despite his mother's old dislike for him, a man who knew his whole past, of his desertion, of his danger,—a man who was himself about enlisting for service in the Philippines, and who persuaded him that his surest way to win exemption from punishment was to hasten after the detachment, beat it, if possible, to Manila, and join it there at his own expense.

He still had some hundreds left. They went to San Francisco, where Walter took steamer at once for Honolulu to await there the coming of the recruit detachment. The infantry finally came, his friend with them, but no sign of more cavalry. To Walter's dismay he had seen among the passengers landed from the Doric the disguised rough whom, as Sackett, he had so unfavorably known before, who as Murray had followed him into the army. It would never do to fall into his clutches again: the man would betray him instantly. Walter kept in hiding until he heard that Sackett was accused of stabbing a staff officer of General Vinton and had fled the island.

Later, when the next troop-ship came, bringing his friend with it, he again took counsel. As the lad fully admitted, his friend was the same old chum of Freiburg days—the friend to whom his parents had so much objected. The fortunes of war had thrown them together, Willard as impecunious as ever, and the Damon and Pythias, the Orestes and Pylades, the two Ajaxes of the old days were in close and intimate touch once more, Damon, as of old, the banker for the twain. The troop-ships were to proceed as soon as coaled. There were reasons now why Walter wished to stay in Honolulu, but Willard urged his moving at once on to Hong Kong and there awaiting the result of his negotiations at Manila. At Hong Kong it was his hope to receive the word "Come over. All is well," and, finally, as his funds would soon run out, he closed his letter with the request that his mother cable him five hundred dollars through the Hong Kong and Shanghai Bank.

The money she cabled at once, then in dread she had wired Colonel Martindale, who was gadding about with old army chums when most she needed him at home, and that gentleman, with a sigh, again went sisterward, saying he knew the boy was sure to turn up to torment him, and wondering what on earth young Hopeful had done now. He looked grave enough when he read the letter, asked for time to communicate confidentially with a chum at Washington, and was awaiting reply when all on a sudden the papers came out with this startling despatch telling of the murder of Private Walter Foster while on his post as sentry at Manila, and then came weeks of woe.

Despite Drayton's cable from Manila that the identification of the remains was not conclusive to him, at least, Mrs. Foster was convinced that the murdered lad was her only boy, and all because of that heartless flirt, that designing— that demoniac army girl who had bewitched him and then brought his blood upon her own head.

"If it isn't Walter who lies there slain by assassin rival, the innocent victim of *that creature's* hideous vanity, would I not have heard from him? Do you suppose my blessed boy would not *instantly* have cabled to tell me he was alive if he wasn't dead?" And, indeed, that was a hard question to answer.

And so the remains of Private Willard Benton, that had been viewed by many a genuinely sorrowing comrade and stowed away with solemn military honors in a vault at Paco Cemetery, were sealed up as best they could do it at Manila, and, though unconvinced as to their identity despite the convictions of others in authority, the commanding general yielded to cables from the War Department and ordered their shipment to San Francisco. They were out of sight of all signals from Corregidor when Martindale's cable came suggesting search for Private Benton Willard.

Zenobia Perkins sniffed contemptuously and scoffed malignantly when told that the doubting Thomases were gaining ground and numbers, that though Mr. Stuyvesant might be brought to trial for killing a man, it would not be for killing Foster until more was ascertained regarding the actual victim. Private Connelly, recovered from his fever, was forever hunting up Farnham, the brakeman, and devising schemes for the capture of that blackguard Murray. Day and night, he maintained that Murray was the man who had accosted Clarke and Hunter at the battery, that it was probably he who, with his pals, had waylaid and robbed the lone recruit returning from his quest in East Paco, that it was he who must have struggled with him again before firing the fatal shot; but not a trace of Murray or his sailor mates could the secret service agents find, and matters were in this most unsatisfactory state when at the end of November came the Queen of the Fleet, despatched several weeks before to fetch along the troops "sidetracked" at Honolulu, just as the commanding general and his chief surgeon were in consultation as to what on earth to do with Zenobia Perkins—the woman had become a public nuisance.

It seems that the Patriotic Daughters of America were now out of patience and the vice-president out of funds. It seemed that her brief ascendancy had carried the lady to such an altitude as to dizzy her brain and rob her of all sense of proportion. It seems that the surgeons in charge of three hospitals had complained of her meddling, that colonels of several regiments had discovered her to be the author of letters to the home papers setting forth that neglect, abuse, and starvation were driving their men to desertion or the grave. It seems that the Red Cross had protested against her as the originator of malignant stories at their expense, and it was evidently high time to get rid of her, yet how could they if that case was to be tried? Zenobia Perkins knew they could not and conducted herself accordingly. She came this day to the Ayuntamiento to demand pay for what she termed her long detention at Manila.

"You compel me to remain against my will because I'm an indispensable witness," said she to the saturnine adjutant-general, beyond whom she never now succeeded in passing. She was volubly berating him, to his grim amusement, when the lattice doors from the corridor swung open and two officers entered.

For nearly two minutes they stood waiting for a break in her tempestuous flow of words, but as none came, the senior impatiently stepped forward and the adjutant-general, looking up, sprang from his chair just as the chief himself came hurrying out from the *sanctum sanctorum* and greeted the newcomers with cordially clasping hands. The lady too had risen. This was another of those stuck-up star-wearers who at San Francisco as much as told her she was a nuisance, and who wouldn't send her by transport to Manila. Yet here she was in spite of them all, and the most important woman on the island! Zenobia's face was flushed with triumph that the star-wearer should be made to feel and see before she would consent to leave the room.

"Well, I shall have to interrupt you gentlemen," said she, "for *my* business won't keep if you propose to keep *me*. I want to know right here and now, General Drayton, whether I'm to get my pay or not; if not, I don't propose to wait another day in Manila, and you can get out of the scrape the best way you know how. No one here but me could swear that young man Foster was dead, and you know it."

"You've sworn to what isn't so, madame," interposed the new arrival placidly. "Here's that young man Foster!" and as he spoke the lattice doors again swung open, and, very pale, a tall youth in civilian dress was ushered in, at sight of whom Major Farquhar fairly shouted.

* * * * *

"How'd I get him?" said the new-comer five minutes later. "Found him aboard the Coptic when she met us as we were pulling out from Honolulu. He was going back to the States. Left Hong Kong before the story was published. Didn't want to come, of course, but had to."

"Wasn't there time to write his mother? They surely would have cabled, and the Coptic must have got into San Francisco a week ago."

"Certainly! Letter was sent right on by the steamer, addressed to Cincinnati."

"O Lord!" said Drayton. "And she was at 'Frisco all the time. Colonel," he added to his chief-of-staff, "what's the first transport home?"

"Zealandia, sir; to-morrow."

"Sorry for the Zealandia, but Zenobia must go with her."

CHAPTER XX

Of course we had not heard the last of her. Honolulu correspondents of the press had little to write of in those days, but made their little long, and Zenobia's stories were the biggest things yet brought from Manila. Those stories were seven days getting from Honolulu to San Francisco, which was less than half the time it took their author to bring them to listening ears. Anybody aboard the Zealandia could have told the scribes the lady was a fabricator of the first magnitude, but what live correspondent wants to have a good story spoiled? In just twenty-seven days from that on which Zenobia bade farewell to Manila her winged words were flashed all over the States, and by thousands were the stones swallowed that death, disease, pestilence and famine, bribery and corruption, vice and debauchery, desertion and demoralization ran riot in the army at Manila, all due to the incapacity, if not actual complicity, of officers in high position. But mercifully were they spared the knowledge of these astonishing facts until the papers themselves began to reach the Eighth Corps some ten weeks after Zenobia had left it to its fate, and by that time every fellow had his hands full, for the long-looked-for outbreak had come at last, and the long, thin Yankee fighting line was too busy making history to waste ink or temper in denying yarns that, after all, were soon forgotten.

Charles King

Then, too, we had been hearing stories that could not be denied right there in the southern suburbs, and having excitement that needed no Zenobia to enhance it. To begin with, Walter Foster's tale was of itself of vivid interest, and, though only the general and Farquhar and Ray actually heard it, and only two or possibly three staff officers were supposed to see it after it had been reduced to writing, every steamer and transport now was bringing officers' families, and men must tell their wives something once in a while, otherwise they might never know what *is* going on and so will believe all manner of things that are not.

Walter Foster's mother learned by cable that the remains she awaited, and that reached port almost the day she got the despatch, were not those of her only son, but of one who had practically died for him. And even in the joy of that supreme moment the woman in her turned, after all, in pity to weep for the motherless lad who had been her boy's warmest friend in his hours of doubt and darkness and despair.

A weak vessel was "Wally," as Farquhar had intimated, and so easily cowed and daunted that in the dread of the punishment accorded the deserter he had skulked in disguise at Hong Kong, leaving all the burden of scouting, pleading, and planning for him to Willard, his old-time chum, who had even less knowledge and experience of army official life than himself. Willard's early letters to Hong Kong gave Foster little hope, for at first the only people the recruit could "sound" were private soldiers like himself. Then Foster read of the arrival of the Sacramento at Manila, of the presence there of Maidie Ray, and then he wrote urging his quondam chum to endeavor to see her, to tell her of his desperate straits, to implore her to exert influence to get him pardoned, and, in order that she might know that his envoy was duly accredited, he sent Willard his chief treasure, that little *carte-de-visite*, together with a few imploring lines.

Then not a word came from Willard for three mortal weeks, but Foster's daily visits to the bank were at last rewarded by a despatch from home bidding him return at once by first steamer, sending him abundant means, and assuring him all would be well.

And when the news of his own murder was published in the Hong Kong papers, without the faintest intimation to the officials of the bank as to his intentions, he was homeward bound, and never heard a word of it all until recognized by an officer aboard the Queen as the Coptic floated into Honolulu Harbor. There he was arrested and turned back.

Among "Billy Benton's" few effects no letters, no such picture, had been found, nothing, in fact, to connect him with Foster. Colonel Brent knew what had become of the *carte-de-visite*, but—how happened it in other hands than those of Benton? That too was not long to be a mystery.

One day in late December a forlorn-looking fellow begged a drink of the bartender at the Alhambra on the Escolta—said he was out of money, deserted by his friends, and took occasion to remind the dispenser of fluid refreshment that a few weeks ago when he had funds and friends both he had spent many a dollar there. The bartender waved him away.

"Awe, give the feller a drink," said boys in blue, in the largeness of their nature and the language of the ranks. "What'll you take, Johnny? Have one with us," and one of the managers hastened over and whispered to some of the flannel-shirted squad, but to no purpose.

The "boys" were bent on benevolence, and "beat" though he might be, the gaunt stranger was made welcome, shared their meat and drink, and, growing speedily confidential in his cups, told them that he could tell a tale some folks would pay well to hear, and then proceeded to stiffen out in a fit.

This brought to mind the event on the Bagumbayan, and somebody said it was "the same feller if not the same fit," and it wouldn't do to leave him there. They took him along in their cab and across to their barracks by the Puente Colgante, and a doctor ministered to him, for it was plain the poor fellow was in sore plight, and a few days later a story worth the telling was going the rounds. The good chaplain of the Californians had heard his partial confession and urged him to tell the whole truth, and that night the last vestige of the crumbling case against Gerard Stuyvesant came tumbling to earth, and Connelly, from the Cuartel de Meisic, nearly ran his sturdy legs off to find Farnham and tell him the tale.

"My real name," said the broken man, "is of no consequence to anybody. I soldiered nearly ten years ago in the Seventh Cavalry, but that fight at Wounded Knee was too much for my nerve, and the boys made life a burden to me afterwards. I 'took on' in another regiment after I skipped from the Seventh, but luck was against me. We were sent to Fort Meade, and there was a gambler in Deadwood, Sackett by name, who had been a few months in the Seventh, but got bob-tailed out for some dirty work, and he knew me at once and swore he'd give me away if I didn't steer fellows up against his game after pay-day. I had to do it, but Captain Ray got onto it all and broke up the scheme and ran Sackett off the reservation, and then he blew on me and I had to quit again. He shot a man over cards, for he was a devil when in drink, and had to clear out, and we met again in Denver. 'Each could give the other away by that time,' said he, and so we joined partnership."

The rest was soon told. Sackett got a job on young Foster's ranch and fell into some further trouble. But when the war came all of them were enlisted, Foster and Sackett in the regulars and he in the First Colorado, but they discharged him at Manila because he had fits, and that gave him a good deal of money for a few days, travel pay home, and all that. Then who should turn up but Sackett with "money to burn" and a scheme to make more. They hired a room in Ermita, and next thing he knew Sackett and some sailor men held up and robbed a soldier, and Sackett was in a tearing rage because no money-belt was found on him. They only got some letters, that little photograph, and perhaps forty dollars "Mex." The photograph he recognized at once,—his former captain's daughter,—and he begged for it and kept it about him until one evening he was taken with another fit, and when he came to the picture was gone.

That night he found Sackett nearly crazy drunk at their lodgings in Ermita. They had a Filipino boy to wait on them then, and Sackett had told the boy where he could find money and jewelry while the family were at dinner around at Colonel Brent's. The boy was willing enough; he was an expert. But he came back scared through; said that the soldiers were close after him. He had some jewelry and a pretty revolver. Sackett told him to keep the jewelry, but took the watch and pistol, and that night the sentries and patrols were searching everywhere, and Sackett and the sailors said they must get away somehow. They drank some more, and finally thought they had a good chance just after the patrol left, and the sentry was talking to an officer on the Calle Real.

They sneaked downstairs and out into the Faura, and there Sackett ran right into the soldier's arms. There was a short, terrible battle, the soldier against Sackett and his sailor friend. The sailor got the sentry's gun away, and Sackett and he wrestled as far as the corner, when there was a shot; the soldier dropped all in a heap and Sackett and the sailor ran for their lives around the corner,—the last he had ever seen or heard of them up to this moment.

So that was how poor Maidie's pistol happened to be picked up on the Calle Real and why one or two assertive officers lately connected with the provost-marshal's and secret-service department concluded that it might be well for them to try regimental duty awhile. That was how it happened, too, that Lieutenant Stuyvesant was prevailed on to take a short leave and run over to Hong Kong. But he came back in a hurry, for there was need of every man and trouble imminent "at the front."

The dawn of that memorable February day had come that saw Manila girdled by the flame of forty thousand rifles and shrouded in the smoke that drifted from the burning roofs of outlying villages from whose walls, windows, and church towers the insurgent islanders had poured their pitiless fire upon the ranks of the American soldiery.

In front of a stone-walled enclosure bordering the principal street in an eastward suburb two or three officers were in earnest consultation. From the ambulance close at hand the attendants were carefully lifting some sorely wounded men. Up the street farther east several little parties coming slowly, haltingly from the front, told that the incessant crash and rattle of musketry in that direction was no mere *feu-de-joie*, while every now and then the angry spat of the steel-clad Mauser on the stony road, the whiz and whirr about the ears of the few who for duty's sake or that of example held their ground in the highway, gave evidence that the Tagal marksmen had their eyes on every visible group of Americans.

In the side streets at right angles to the main thoroughfare reserve battalions were crouching, sheltered from the leaden storm, and awaiting the longed-for order to advance and sweep the field at the front. From the grim, gray walls of the great church and convent, which for weeks had been strictly guarded by order of the American generals against all possible intrusion or desecration on part of their men, came frequent flash and report and deadly missile aimed at the helpless wounded, the hurrying ambulances, even at a symbol as sacred as that which towered above its altars—the blood-red cross of Geneva.

It was the Tagal's return for the honor and care and consideration shown the Church of Rome. As another ambulance came swiftly to the spot, its driver swayed, clasped his hands upon his breast, and, with the blood gushing from his mouth, toppled forward into the arms of the hospital attendants. It was more than flesh and blood or the brigade commander could stand.

"Burn that church!" was the stern order as the general spurred on to the front, and a score of soldiers, leaping from behind the stone walls, dashed at the barricaded doors. A young staff officer, galloping down the road, reined in at sight of the little party and whirled about by the general's side.

"It's perfectly true, sir," said he. "Right across the bridge in front of the block-house you can hear him plainly. It's a white man giving orders to the Filipinos." The general nodded.

"We'll get him presently. Do they understand the orders on the left?"

"Everywhere, sir. All are ready and eager," and even the native pony ridden by the aide seemed quivering with excitement as, horse and rider, they fell back and joined the two officers following their chief.

"Hot in front, Stuyvie?" queried the first in undertone, as a Mauser zipped between their heads to the detriment of confidential talk, and a great burst of cheers broke from the blue line crouching just ahead across the open field. "Why, d—n it, man, you're hit now!"

"Hush!" answered Stuyvesant imploringly, as he pressed a gauntleted hand to his side. "Don't let the general know. I want to join Vinton in a moment. It's only a tear along the skin." But blood was soaking through the serge of his blue sack-coat and streaking the loose folds of his riding-breeches, and the bright color in his clear skin was giving way to pallor.

"Tear, indeed! Here! Quick, orderly! Help me there on the other side!" and the captain sprang from saddle. A soldier leaped forward, turning loose his pony, and as the general, with only one aide and orderly, rode on into the smoke-cloud overhanging the line, Gerard Stuyvesant, fainting, slid forward into the arms of his faithful friends.

A few hours later, "lined up" along the river-bank, a great regiment from the far West, panting and exultant, stood resting on its arms and looking back over the field traversed in its first grand charge. Here, there, everywhere it was strewn with insurgent dead and sorely wounded. Here, there, and everywhere men in American blue were flitting about from group to group, tendering canteens of cold water to the wounded, friend and enemy alike.

Far back towards the dusty highway where the ambulances were hurrying, and close to the abutments of a massive stone bridge that crossed a tributary of the Pasig, three officers, a surgeon, and half-a-dozen soldiers were grouped about a prostrate form in the pale blue uniform, with the gold embroidery and broad stripes of a Filipino captain, but the face was ghastly white, the language ghastly Anglo-Saxon.

With the blood welling from a shothole in his broad, burly chest and the seal of death already settling on his ashen brow, he was scowling up into the half-compassionate, half-contemptuous faces about him. Here lay the *"Capitan Americano"* of whom the Tagal soldiers had been boasting for a month—a deserter from the army of the United States, a commissioned officer in the ranks of Aguinaldo, shot to death in his first battle in sight of some who had seen and known him "in the blue."

Lieutenant Stuyvesant, revived by a long pull at the doctor's flask, his bleeding stanched, had again pressed forward to take his part in the fight, but now lay back in the low Victoria that the men had run forward from the village, and looked down upon the man who in bitter wrath and hatred had vowed long months before to have his heart's blood,— the man who had so nearly done him to death in Honolulu. Even now in Sackett's dying eyes something of the same brutal rage mingled with the instant gleam of recognition that for a moment flashed across his distorted features. It seemed retribution indeed that his last conscious glance should fall upon the living face of the man to whom he owed his rescue from a fearful death that night in far-away Nevada.

But, badly as he was whipped that brilliant Sunday, "Johnny Filipino" had the wit to note that Uncle Sam had hardly a handful of cavalry and nowhere near enough men to follow up the advantages, and hence the long campaign of minor affairs that had to follow. In that campaign Sandy Ray was far too busy at the front to know very much of what was going on at the rear in Manila. He listened with little sympathy to Farquhar's brief disposition of poor Foster's case. "They could remove the desertion and give him a commission, but they couldn't make Wally a soldier. He went home when the fighting had hardly begun." Somebody was mean enough to say if he hadn't his mother would have come for him.

There was no question as to the identity of the soldier who died in Filipino uniform. Not only did Stuyvesant recognize him, but so did Ray and Trooper Mellen, and Connelly, fetched over from the north side to make assurance doubly sure. It was Sackett-Murray, gambler, horse-thief, house-robber, deserter, biter, murderer, and double-dyed traitor. He had fled to the insurgents in dread of discovery and death at the hands of Benton's comrades.

And perhaps it was just as well. Foster knew of his hapless end before he took steamer homeward; knew, too, of Stuyvesant's wound, and—possibly it had something to do with his departure—of the disposition made of that fortunately wounded officer. Miss Ray, it seems, was regularly on duty now, with other Red Cross nurses, and Stuyvesant went to the "First Reserve" and stayed there a whole week, and even Dr. Wells came and smiled on him, and Miss Porter beamed, and still he was not happy—for Maidie came not. She was busy as she could be at the farther end of the other wards.

And so Stuyvesant grew impatient of nursing, declared he was well, and still was far from happy, for at that time Foster was still hovering about the premises, and Stuyvesant could see only one possible explanation for that. They moved him back to his breezy quarters at Malate. But presently a trap was sprung, mainly through Mrs. Brent's complicity, for once or twice a week it was Maidie's custom to go to her old friend's roof for rest and tea. And one evening, seems to me it was Valentine's Day, just before sunset, they were in the veranda,—the colonel and his kindly wife,—while Maid Marion the Second was in her own room donning a dainty gown for change from the Red Cross uniform, when a carriage whirled up to the entrance underneath, and Mrs. Brent, leaning over the rail, smiled on its sole occupant and nodded reassuringly.

Stuyvesant came up slowly, looking not too robust, and said it was awfully good of Mrs. Brent to take pity on his loneliness and have him round to tea. Other nice women, younger, more attractive personally than Mrs. Brent, had likewise bidden him to tea just so soon as he felt able, but Stuyvesant swore to himself he couldn't be able and wouldn't if he could. Yet when Mrs. Brent said "Come," he went, though never hoping to see Marion, whom he believed to be engrossed in duties at the First Reserve, and on the verge of announcement of her engagement to "that young man Foster."

Presently Brent said if Stuyvesant had no objection he'd take his trap and drive over *Intra muros* and get the news from MacArthur's front,—for Mac was hammering at the insurgent lines about Caloocan,—and Stuyvesant had no objection whatever. Whereupon Mrs. Brent took occasion to say in the most casual way in the world:

"Oh, you might send a line to Colonel Martindale, dear. You know Mr. Foster goes home by the Sonoma—oh, hadn't you heard of it, Mr. Stuyvesant? Oh, dear, yes. He's been ready to go ever since the fighting began, but there was no boat."

And then she too left Stuyvesant,—left him with the New York *Moon* bottom topmost in his hand and a sensation as of wheels in his head. She proceeded, furthermore, to order tea on the back gallery and Maidie to the front. But tea was ready long before Maidie.

Far out at the lines of San Pedro Macati Dyer's guns had sighted swarms of rebels up the Pasig, and with placid and methodical precision were sending shrapnel in that direction and dull, booming concussions in the other. An engagement of some kind was on at San Pedro, and Stuyvesant twitched with nervous longing to get there, despite the doctors, and sat wondering was another engagement off at Manila. Just what to do he had not decided. The *Moon* and his senses were still upside-down when Sing came in with the transferred tea things and Mrs. Brent with the last thing Stuyvesant was thinking to see—Maid Marion, all smiles, congratulation, and cool organdie.

Ten minutes' time in which to compose herself gives a girl far too great an advantage under such circumstances.

"I—I'm glad to see you," said Stuyvesant helplessly. "I thought you were wearing yourself out at nursing."

"Oh, it agrees with me," responded Maidie blithely.

"I suppose it must. You certainly look so."

"*Merci du compliment, Monsieur,*" smiled Miss Ray, with sparkling eyes and the prettiest of courtesies. She certainly did look remarkably well.

It was time for Stuyvesant to be seated again, but he hovered there about that tea-table, for Mrs. Brent made the totally unnecessary announcement that she would go in search of the spoons.

"You had no time—I suppose—to look in on anybody but your assigned vict—patients, I mean," hazarded Stuyvesant, weakening his tentative by palpable display of sense of injury.

"Well, you were usually asleep when I cal—inquired, I mean. One or two lumps, Mr. Stuyvesant?" And the dainty little white hand hovered over the sugar-bowl.

"You usually chose such times, I fancy. One lump, thanks." There was another, not of sugar, in his throat and he knew it, and his fine blue eyes and thin, sad face were pathetic enough to move any woman's heart had not Miss Ray been so concerned about the tea.

"You would have been able to return to duty days ago," said she, tendering the steaming cup and obviously ignoring his remark, "had you come right to hospital as Dr. Shiels directed, instead of scampering out to the front again. You thought more of the brevet, of course, than the gash. What a mercy it glanced on the rib! Only—such wounds are ever so much harder to stanch and dress."

"You—knew about it, then?" he asked with reviving hope.

"Of course. We *all* knew," responded Miss Ray, well aware of the fact that he would have been unaccountably and infinitely happier had it been she alone. "That is our profession. But about the brevet. Surely you ought to be pleased. Captain in your first engagement!"

"Oh, it's only a recommendation," he answered, "and may be as far away as—any other engagement—of mine, that is." And in saying it poor Stuyvesant realized it was an asinine thing. So, alack, did she! An instant agone she was biting her pretty red lips for letting the word escape her, but his fatuity gave her all the advantage in spite of herself. It was the play to see nothing that called for reply in his allusion. So there was none.

A carriage was coming up the Luneta full tilt, and though still six hundred yards away, she saw and knew it to be Stuyvesant's returning. But he saw nothing beyond her glowing face. Mrs. Brent began to sing in the salon, a symptom so unusual that it could only mean that she contemplated coming back and was giving warning. Time was priceless, yet here he stood trembling, irresolute. Would nothing help him?

"You speak of my—engagement," he blundered blindly on. "I wish you'd tell me—about yours."

"Mine? Oh,—with the Red Cross, you mean? And shame be to you, Maidie Ray, you knew—you well knew—he didn't."

"I mean—to Mr. Foster. Mrs. Brent has just told me—"

"Mrs. Brent!" interposes Miss Ray in a flutter of amaze. That carriage is coming nearer every instant, driving like mad, Brent on the back seat and a whip-lashing demon on the box. There will be no time for love-tales once that burly warrior returns to his own. Yet she is fencing, parrying, holding him at bay, for his heart is bubbling over with the torrent of its love and yearning and pleading.

What are bullet-wounds and brevets to this one supreme, sublime encounter? His heart was high, his voice rang clear and exultant, his eyes flashed joy and fire and defiance in the face of a thousand deaths two weeks ago. But here in the presence of a slender girl he can do naught but falter and stammer and tremble.

Crack, crack, spatter, clatter, and crash comes the little carriage and team whirling into the San Luis. He hears it now. He knows what it means to him—Brent back and the pent-up words still unspoken! It nerves him to the test, it spurs him to the leap, it drives the blood bounding through his veins, it sends him darting round the table to her side, penning her, as it were, between him and the big bamboo chair. And now her heart, too, is all in a flutter, for the outer works were carried in his impetuous dash, the assailant is at the very citadel.

"Marion!" he cried, "tell me, was there—tell me, there *was* no engagement! Tell me there *is* a little hope for me! Oh, you are blind if you do not see, if you *have* not seen all along, that I've loved you ever since the first day I ever saw you. Tell me—quick!"

Too late. Up comes Brent on the run, and Marion springs past the would-be detaining arm. "Where's Mrs. B.?" pants the warrior. "Hullo, Stuyvie! I was afraid you'd got the news and gone out in a cab. M'ria, I want my belt and pistol!"

"*Where* you going?" bursts in the lady of the house—the spoons forgotten.

"Out to San Pedro! It's only three miles. Our fellows are going to drive 'em out of Guadaloupe woods. Ready, Sty? Of course you want to see it. Drive'll do you good, too. Come on."

"Indeed, you don't stir a step, Colonel Brent!—not a step! What business have you going into action? You did enough fighting forty years ago." Brent, deaf to her expostulation, is rushing to the steps, buckling his belt on the run, but "M'ria" grabs the slack of the Khaki coat and holds him. Stuyvesant springs for his hat. It has vanished. Marion, her hands behind her, her lips parted, her heart pounding hard, has darted to the broad door to the salon, and there, leaning against the framing, she confronts him.

At the rear of the salon Thisbe has grappled Pyramus and is being pulled to the head of the stairs; at the head, Beatrice, with undaunted front, concealing a sinking heart, defies Benedick.

"My hat, please," he demands, his eyes lighting with hope and promise of victory.

"You have no right," she begins. "You are still a patient." But now, with bowed head, she is struggling, for he has come close to her, so close that his heart and hers might almost meet in their wild leaping, so close that in audacious search for the missing headgear his hands are reaching down behind the shrinking, slender little form, and his long, sinewy arms almost encircling her. The war of words at the back stairs "now trebly thundering swelled the gale," but it is not heard here at the front.

His hands have grasped her wrists now. His blond head is bowed down over hers, so that his lips hover close to the part of the dusky hair. "My hat, Maidie," he cries, "or I'll—I'll take what I want!" Both hands tugging terrifically at those slender wrists now, and yet not gaining an inch. "Do you hear?—I'll—I'll take—"

"You sha'n't!" gasps Miss Ray, promptly burying her glowing face in the breast of that happy Khaki, and thereby tacitly admitting that she knows just what he wants so much more than that hat.

And then the long, white hands release their hold of the slim, white wrists; the muscular arms twine tight about her, almost lifting her from her feet; the bonny brown head bows lower still, his mustache brushing the soft, damask-rose-like cheek. "I must go, Maidie,—darling!" he whispers, "without the hat if need be, but not without—this—and this—and this—and this," and the last one lingers long just at the corner of the warm, winsome, rosy lips. She could not prevent it—perhaps she did not try.

Choose from Thousands of 1stWorldLibrary Classics By

A. M. Barnard
Ada Leverson
Adolphus William Ward
Aesop
Agatha Christie
Alexander Aaronsohn
Alexander Kielland
Alexandre Dumas
Alfred Gatty
Alfred Ollivant
Alice Duer Miller
Alice Turner Curtis
Alice Dunbar
Allen Chapman
Alleyne Ireland
Ambrose Bierce
Amelia E. Barr
Amory H. Bradford
Andrew Lang
Andrew McFarland Davis
Andy Adams
Angela Brazil
Anna Alice Chapin
Anna Sewell
Annie Besant
Annie Hamilton Donnell
Annie Payson Call
Annie Roe Carr
Annonaymous
Anton Chekhov
Archibald Lee Fletcher
Arnold Bennett
Arthur C. Benson
Arthur Conan Doyle
Arthur M. Winfield
Arthur Ransome
Arthur Schnitzler
Arthur Train
Atticus
B.H. Baden-Powell
B. M. Bower
B. C. Chatterjee
Baroness Emmuska Orczy
Baroness Orczy
Basil King
Bayard Taylor
Ben Macomber
Bertha Muzzy Bower
Bjornstjerne Bjornson

Booth Tarkington
Boyd Cable
Bram Stoker
C. Collodi
C. E. Orr
C. M. Ingleby
Carolyn Wells
Catherine Parr Traill
Charles A. Eastman
Charles Amory Beach
Charles Dickens
Charles Dudley Warner
Charles Farrar Browne
Charles Ives
Charles Kingsley
Charles Klein
Charles Hanson Towne
Charles Lathrop Pack
Charles Romyn Dake
Charles Whibley
Charles Willing Beale
Charlotte M. Braeme
Charlotte M. Yonge
Charlotte Perkins Stetson
Clair W. Hayes
Clarence Day Jr.
Clarence E. Mulford
Clemence Housman
Confucius
Coningsby Dawson
Cornelis DeWitt Wilcox
Cyril Burleigh
D. H. Lawrence
Daniel Defoe
David Garnett
Dinah Craik
Don Carlos Janes
Donald Keyhoe
Dorothy Kilner
Dougan Clark
Douglas Fairbanks
E. Nesbit
E. P. Roe
E. Phillips Oppenheim
E. S. Brooks
Earl Barnes
Edgar Rice Burroughs
Edith Van Dyne
Edith Wharton

Edward Everett Hale
Edward J. O'Biren
Edward S. Ellis
Edwin L. Arnold
Eleanor Atkins
Eleanor Hallowell Abbott
Eliot Gregory
Elizabeth Gaskell
Elizabeth McCracken
Elizabeth Von Arnim
Ellem Key
Emerson Hough
Emilie F. Carlen
Emily Bronte
Emily Dickinson
Enid Bagnold
Enilor Macartney Lane
Erasmus W. Jones
Ernie Howard Pie
Ethel May Dell
Ethel Turner
Ethel Watts Mumford
Eugene Sue
Eugenie Foa
Eugene Wood
Eustace Hale Ball
Evelyn Everett-green
Everard Cotes
F. H. Cheley
F. J. Cross
F. Marion Crawford
Fannie E. Newberry
Federick Austin Ogg
Ferdinand Ossendowski
Fergus Hume
Florence A. Kilpatrick
Fremont B. Deering
Francis Bacon
Francis Darwin
Frances Hodgson Burnett
Frances Parkinson Keyes
Frank Gee Patchin
Frank Harris
Frank Jewett Mather
Frank L. Packard
Frank V. Webster
Frederic Stewart Isham
Frederick Trevor Hill
Frederick Winslow Taylor

Friedrich Kerst
Friedrich Nietzsche
Fyodor Dostoyevsky
G.A. Henty
G.K. Chesterton
Gabrielle E. Jackson
Garrett P. Serviss
Gaston Leroux
George A. Warren
George Ade
Geroge Bernard Shaw
George Cary Eggleston
George Durston
George Ebers
George Eliot
George Gissing
George MacDonald
George Meredith
George Orwell
George Sylvester Viereck
George Tucker
George W. Cable
George Wharton James
Gertrude Atherton
Gordon Casserly
Grace E. King
Grace Gallatin
Grace Greenwood
Grant Allen
Guillermo A. Sherwell
Gulielma Zollinger
Gustav Flaubert
H. A. Cody
H. B. Irving
H.C. Bailey
H. G. Wells
H. H. Munro
H. Irving Hancock
H. R. Naylor
H. Rider Haggard
H. W. C. Davis
Haldeman Julius
Hall Caine
Hamilton Wright Mabie
Hans Christian Andersen
Harold Avery
Harold McGrath
Harriet Beecher Stowe
Harry Castlemon
Harry Coghill
Harry Houidini

Hayden Carruth
Helent Hunt Jackson
Helen Nicolay
Hendrik Conscience
Hendy David Thoreau
Henri Barbusse
Henrik Ibsen
Henry Adams
Henry Ford
Henry Frost
Henry James
Henry Jones Ford
Henry Seton Merriman
Henry W Longfellow
Herbert A. Giles
Herbert Carter
Herbert N. Casson
Herman Hesse
Hildegard G. Frey
Homer
Honore De Balzac
Horace B. Day
Horace Walpole
Horatio Alger Jr.
Howard Pyle
Howard R. Garis
Hugh Lofting
Hugh Walpole
Humphry Ward
Ian Maclaren
Inez Haynes Gillmore
Irving Bacheller
Isabel Cecilia Williams
Isabel Hornibrook
Israel Abrahams
Ivan Turgenev
J.G.Austin
J. Henri Fabre
J. M. Barrie
J. M. Walsh
J. Macdonald Oxley
J. R. Miller
J. S. Fletcher
J. S. Knowles
J. Storer Clouston
J. W. Duffield
Jack London
Jacob Abbott
James Allen
James Andrews
James Baldwin

James Branch Cabell
James DeMille
James Joyce
James Lane Allen
James Lane Allen
James Oliver Curwood
James Oppenheim
James Otis
James R. Driscoll
Jane Abbott
Jane Austen
Jane L. Stewart
Janet Aldridge
Jens Peter Jacobsen
Jerome K. Jerome
Jessie Graham Flower
John Buchan
John Burroughs
John Cournos
John F. Kennedy
John Gay
John Glasworthy
John Habberton
John Joy Bell
John Kendrick Bangs
John Milton
John Philip Sousa
John Taintor Foote
Jonas Lauritz Idemil Lie
Jonathan Swift
Joseph A. Altsheler
Joseph Carey
Joseph Conrad
Joseph E. Badger Jr
Joseph Hergesheimer
Joseph Jacobs
Jules Vernes
Julian Hawthrone
Julie A Lippmann
Justin Huntly McCarthy
Kakuzo Okakura
Karle Wilson Baker
Kate Chopin
Kenneth Grahame
Kenneth McGaffey
Kate Langley Bosher
Kate Langley Bosher
Katherine Cecil Thurston
Katherine Stokes
L. A. Abbot
L. T. Meade

L. Frank Baum	Owen Johnson	Stephen Crane
Latta Griswold	P.G. Wodehouse	Stewart Edward White
Laura Dent Crane	Paul and Mabel Thorne	Stijn Streuvels
Laura Lee Hope	Paul G. Tomlinson	Swami Abhedananda
Laurence Housman	Paul Severing	Swami Parmananda
Lawrence Beasley	Percy Brebner	T. S. Ackland
Leo Tolstoy	Percy Keese Fitzhugh	T. S. Arthur
Leonid Andreyev	Peter B. Kyne	The Princess Der Ling
Lewis Carroll	Plato	Thomas A. Janvier
Lewis Sperry Chafer	Quincy Allen	Thomas A Kempis
Lilian Bell	R. Derby Holmes	Thomas Anderton
Lloyd Osbourne	R. L. Stevenson	Thomas Bailey Aldrich
Louis Hughes	R. S. Ball	Thomas Bulfinch
Louis Joseph Vance	Rabindranath Tagore	Thomas De Quincey
Louis Tracy	Rahul Alvares	Thomas Dixon
Louisa May Alcott	Ralph Bonehill	Thomas H. Huxley
Lucy Fitch Perkins	Ralph Henry Barbour	Thomas Hardy
Lucy Maud Montgomery	Ralph Victor	Thomas More
Luther Benson	Ralph Waldo Emmerson	Thornton W. Burgess
Lydia Miller Middleton	Rene Descartes	U. S. Grant
Lyndon Orr	Ray Cummings	Upton Sinclair
M. Corvus	Rex Beach	Valentine Williams
M. H. Adams	Rex E. Beach	Various Authors
Margaret E. Sangster	Richard Harding Davis	Vaughan Kester
Margret Howth	Richard Jefferies	Victor Appleton
Margaret Vandercook	Richard Le Gallienne	Victor G. Durham
Margaret W. Hungerford	Robert Barr	Victoria Cross
Margret Penrose	Robert Frost	Virginia Woolf
Maria Edgeworth	Robert Gordon Anderson	Wadsworth Camp
Maria Thompson Daviess	Robert L. Drake	Walter Camp
Mariano Azuela	Robert Lansing	Walter Scott
Marion Polk Angellotti	Robert Lynd	Washington Irving
Mark Overton	Robert Michael Ballantyne	Wilbur Lawton
Mark Twain	Robert W. Chambers	Wilkie Collins
Mary Austin	Rosa Nouchette Carey	Willa Cather
Mary Catherine Crowley	Rudyard Kipling	Willard F. Baker
Mary Cole	Saint Augustine	William Dean Howells
Mary Hastings Bradley	Samuel B. Allison	William le Queux
Mary Roberts Rinehart	Samuel Hopkins Adams	W. Makepeace Thackeray
Mary Rowlandson	Sarah Bernhardt	William W. Walter
M. Wollstonecraft Shelley	Sarah C. Hallowell	William Shakespeare
Maud Lindsay	Selma Lagerlof	Winston Churchill
Max Beerbohm	Sherwood Anderson	Yei Theodora Ozaki
Myra Kelly	Sigmund Freud	Yogi Ramacharaka
Nathaniel Hawthrone	Standish O'Grady	Young E. Allison
Nicolo Machiavelli	Stanley Weyman	Zane Grey
O. F. Walton	Stella Benson	
Oscar Wilde	Stella M. Francis